GROWING UP VENICE

GROWING UP VENICE:

PARALLEL UNIVERSES

A History

Narrative-Nonfiction

Venice-of-America

DONNA L. FRIESS, PH.D.

2020

Library of Congress-in-Publication Data
All Rights Reserved
Copyright 2020 by Donna L. Friess

Friess, Donna L.
Growing Up Venice: Parallel Universes
Donna Lewis Friess
   1.   History
Hurt Into Happiness Publishing, 31506 Paseo Christina, San Juan Capistrano, CA 92675

First Edition
   978-0-9815767-7-0
   0-9815767-7-X

This book is a personal history of Venice, California
Printed in the United States of America
Publisher's Cataloguing-in-Publication
Friess, Donna L., 1943-

   Growing Up Venice: Parallel Universes, Donna Friess. -- San Juan Capistrano: Hurt into Happiness Publishing, [2020]

Library of Congress
   Includes bibliography.

   Summary: This work is a collection of historical accountings and oral histories based upon the memories of those contributors described in the bibliography section. It is the history of Venice, California.

Historian Donna Friess, Ph.D. brings Venice, California's vibrant colorful story to life in this personally written narrative based upon interviews, written statements, field trips, as well as historical accountings. The history begins with her family's interest in Venice-of-America from the late 1880's, across time to the discovery of oil, its evolution as an artists' Mecca, its fame as a "must see" tourist attraction, through to the arrival of big tech as Silicon Beach.

To Order books visit Amazon.com. Also available through Kindle Publishing.

Cover: Design by Mariuz Jeglinski.

Books by Donna Friess

Women Leaders of the Movement to Stop Child Sexual Abuse
A Doctoral Dissertation. An Oral History 1992

Cry the Darkness: One Woman's Triumph over the Tragedy of Incest, 1993
2nd Edition, 2013

Whispering Waters: Historic Weesha and the Settling of Southern California (Oral History) With Janet
Tonkovich, 1998

A Chronicle of Historic Weesha and the Upper Santa Ana River Valley
with Janet Tonkovich, 2000.

Circle of Love: A Guide to Successful Relationships, 3rd Edition, 2008

One Hundred Years of Weesha: Centennial 2010. An Oral History, 2010

Cherish the Light: One Woman's Journey from Darkness to Light, 2013

Just Between Us: Guide to Healing (1995, out of print)

The Unraveling of Shelby Forrest 2014 – a Novel

Capistrano Trails: Ride for the Brand, 2018. An Oral History.

True Animal Short Stories for Children:

Oh What a Big Surprise!

Three Little Kittens Lost in the Woodpile

Zoe's First Birthday

There's Something Scary in the Shed

Starving in the Woods

Winning the Horse Race

Jessica the Seal

About Cry the Darkness

Winner Indie Excellence Book Awards – Women's Issues 2014
Honorable Mention – Paris International Book Festival 2014
Honorable Mention – New York Book Festival 2014
Honorable Mention- Southern California Book Festival 2014
Honorable Mention – London International Books Awards 2014
Honorable Mention – New England Festival of Books 2014
"A real contribution to women everywhere." *Changes Magazine.*

Re-released by Bastei Lubbe Publishing. Germany, 2018

"It is a wonderful book!" Marilyn Van Derbur, Former Miss America, incest survivor.

"I couldn't put it down. It is inspirational!" *Alpha Gamma Delta International Quarterly*

"It is a gripping story…it keeps the reader moving." U.S. International University *Envoy.*

"A must read for everyone. One of the most important books available. It gives hope. Donna's life story is a beacon of hope and happiness for adult survivors of sexual abuse." Claire Reeves, Founder, Mothers Against Sexual Abuse.

Cry the Darkness is my most valued possession." Gina, Incest survivor and AIDS patient.

"It changed my life and gave me hope." Sonja, Incest survivor.

"*Tarer I Morket.*" Best selling non-fiction book in the history of Egmont (Virkelightedens Verden) publishing, Norway, 1990's. Egmont Bogklub.

"An inspiration for those working for victims of childhood trauma." *Changes Magazine.*

"Outstanding Donna! A good reminder that we DO have a choice in how we respond." Judy P., Reader.

About The Unraveling of Shelby Forrest

Winner Indie Excellence Book Awards – Best New Novel 2015
Honorable Mention- Pacific Rim International Book Awards 2015
Independent Author Network, IAN- Finalist Book of the Year Awards- Romance 2015
Honorable Mention- Paris International Book Festival 2015
Honorable Mention – New York Book Festival 2015
Honorable Mention – Southern California Book Festival 2016
Honorable Mention – London International Festival of Books 2016
Honorable Mention – Los Angeles Book Festival 2016
Honorable Mention- Hollywood Book Festival 2016

Whispering Water: Historic Weesha and the Settling of Southern California.

Whispering Waters: Historic Weesha and the Settling of Southern California. 1998, 2nd Ed. 2016.
Finalist: International Book Excellence Awards. Non-Fiction. 2017

About *Capistrano Trails: Ride for the Brand*

Capistrano Trails: Ride for the Brand. 2018. Finalist- International Book Excellence- Awards Non-fiction. 2019.

Finalist: Indie Excellent Awards. Non-fiction. 2019.
Finalist: 14th National Next Generation Indie Excellence Awards. Non-fiction. 2020.

This book, *Capistrano Trails* is Donna's valentine to San Juan Capistrano and to horses.

For those who cherish our human story;
And to the visionaries who conceived Los Angeles as a world-
class metropolis in the middle of a California desert;
as well as the hardworking pioneers and
dreamers who made it happen.

ACKNOWLEDGMENTS

This collection of memories and historical accounts would not have been possible without the cooperation and willingness to share on the part of all of my contributors. I appreciate their candid and personal stories. A special thanks to my siblings: Jacqueline R. Lewis, DDS, Dee Dee Lewis Keel, Charles H. Lewis, Ed.D, Diana Lewis Starr, Raymond W. Lewis, III, and Cynthia Lewis Lang. In addition, I am grateful to the Clifton family John, Charlie, and Sherry for their remarkable contributions.

I have relied heavily upon the photographic evidence of life in Venice-of-America, at the turn of the 20th Century, much of which was left to us by our forebearers. I am the recipient of both of my grandparents' and great grandparents' personal mementos and papers. My paternal great grandparents arrived in Los Angeles about 1887 with two small children and the earnest drive to open up pharmacies, which they did. My paternal grandparents were devotees to the amusements at Venice-of-America. My grandmother, Vera-May "Maymie" Cooper Lewis, born in Los Angeles in 1901, especially documented her life through photos at the beach in Venice.

I appreciate my husband, Ken's encouragement about the idea of preserving this slice of lost Los Angeles history. He has always been a great help, but during this trying time of being under national quarantine, his sound thinking was particularly valuable to me in bouncing my ideas around. He always stops to discuss whatever thought is gnawing at me during my writing. Thank you to my sister, Diana Starr, for all of her technical support and her love. Photographer, Mario Jeglinski, created the perfect design on the cover to illustrate what this book is about. His contribution is very much appreciated.

I deeply appreciate my sons, Rick and Dan Friess, and my daughters-in-law Jenny and Natalie, and my daughter, Julina, and my son-in-law Justin Bert, who inspire me to be the best I can be. I have written this history as a reminder to cherish the past for my eleven grandchildren: Jake, Jillian, Megan, Jaycelin, Emily, James, Elizabeth, Ella, Ashley, Kate, and Caroline. I find a deep purpose for living through all of you. Thank you for your faith in me.

TIMELINE VENICE - LOS ANGELES

38,000 B.C.	Animal fossils prehistory.
8000 B.C.	Native People settle in Ballona Wetlands and Los Angeles Basin.
500 A.D.	Tongva People (later known as Gabrielenos) displace earlier people in Ballona Wetlands and Los Angeles Basin.
1542	Cabrillo sails by Southern California near San Pedro and refers to Native Peoples' fires and names the waterfront, "Bay of Smokes."
1771	Mission San Gabriel founded by Spanish missionaries. Mission system established. Population of Indigenous People estimated at 350,000.
1781	Eleven families settle the Pueblo de Los Angles. Population 44.
1820	Machado and Telemendes granted Rancho La Ballona by Spain.
1821	Mexico declares its independence from Spain.
1835	Los Angeles promoted from *pueblo* to territorial *Capital of Alta California*.
1841	The first census shows population of 141 in Los Angeles.
1848	Gold is discovered accidentally in Sutter Creek, in north-eastern California.
1850	Los Angeles City population was 1600. California becomes the 30th state in the United States.
1869	First Transcontinental Railroad.
1885	Santa Fe Railroad brings settlers from the East.
1890	Population is 50,000 in Los Angeles.
1893	After three years of dredging Ballona Wetlands for a harbor, Wicks files for Bankruptcy. Banks fail due to shaky railroad investments. Depression begins.
1897	Los Angeles highly productive oil fields.
1900	Population of Los Angeles 102,000.
1904	Abbot Kinney begins major dredging operation for canals for Venice-of-America.
1905	July 4th Abbot Kinney opens Venice-of-America to crowds of 40,000.
1913	Los Angeles Aqueduct built. Water brought to L.A. from Owens Valley.
1915	55,000 cars on the streets of Los Angeles.

1920	Los Angeles Population reaches half million. Abbot Kinney dies. Fire destroys Venice Pier. Kinney's son, Thornton struggles to find funds to rebuild Venice Pier.
1922-26	Venice canals filling with silt and pollution.
1926	Venice City Council votes to annex to Los Angeles. Canals filled and paved over.
1930	Oil frenzy begins on Venice peninsula and wetlands. LAX opens. Population 1.3 million.
1940	Howard Hughes purchases 400 acres of Ballona Wetlands for his aircraft factory. Builds the factory which operated until 1985.
1945	End of WWII attracts crowds to Venice and Ocean Park Piers.
1946	County of Los Angeles fails to renew Venice Pier lease. Demands pier be removed.
1965	Marina del Rey Opens.
2002	Planned community of Playa Vista opens.
2011	Tech giant, Google, relocates to Main Street in Venice. Tech industry moves in. Property values escalate.
2020	Los Angeles population 12,447,000. California population 40 million.

CONTENTS

Venice is caught in a visible struggle between preserving the past and living in the present. This is a universal cultural struggle. The present after all, is consistently a reflection of its past.

Introduction

My Venice Beach: Rolling Waves, Pumping Oil Wells

Only through trickery and contrivance could the barren corner of
Southern California become a metropolis- Krist (2018)

The adventure which I am inviting you to share, has probably been roiling around inside my brain for decades. Not until the long weeks [as it turns out…long months!!] of the mandatory spring governmental coronavirus lockdown, did my thoughts turn to writing this story for you. After four, seemingly endless, weeks of sheltering-in-place during the Pandemic of 2020, I had already walked my dogs until they looked at me with dull expressions, ridden the horses until one began to limp, and read far too many books. To declare that I was getting restless might be an understatement.

One day, thinking about the extensive genealogy research which my sister, Jackie, had been doing across the past five years, I contacted her. My eager words spilled out. "Sis, you've learned so much about our ancestors. How would it be if you told me some of it and I wrote it down for our kids and grandchildren?"

"Sis, it's too much info."

"Oh." I know my voice carried my disappointment.

She paused a bit and continued. "How about I bring you some materials and set them on your porch? I've gotten through the eighth generation. Maybe you want to take on the challenge of bringing the study up to the present?"

Placing the items on the porch was a safe-guard against the evil and invisible wrath of the COVID-19 disease. I wasn't sure what I'd agreed to, because I was not familiar with genealogy research. I did not know what any of it entailed. I had not seen her materials, but after four weeks of being stuck at home, I cheerfully agreed.

The materials were delivered. They seemed so extensive that they nearly scared me away. It took a few more days to get up my courage to examine them. Clearly, my sister had accomplished the hard part. I dug in and two weeks later I had produced a 20-page summary of our family in the New World from 1634 to 2020. Once I got into the genealogy, I got the hang of it and enjoyed it. Please don't get too excited. I was only summarizing what was before me.

I had my pages printed up, bound, and handed out. That had been satisfying. I took note of the fact that most of the United States was still in lockdown. All the beaches, bike riding trails, parks, and open spaces continued to be closed, as well as were all non-essential businesses. Almost all retail, restaurants and theaters were shutdown. It was odd to discover that two of my favorite things had been going into *non-essential* stores and restaurants! Anyway, the few times I had ventured out to Von's Market to load in groceries, I had seen big electronic signs saying "Save Lives. Stay Home."

I continued to mull over the idea of my ancestors coming west to settle in Los Angeles. It was a project I could do. The family photos of our long-gone relatives enjoying Venice Pier, and the beach front amusements seemed to settle in my hands. My brain was being awakened.

Some of our neighbors dared to drive near the ocean where we live in Orange County. They reported seeing flashing electronic signs: *Go Home*! Those orders, and the loss of personal freedom felt like a noose around my neck. We still had weeks to go; our state was not ready to open up. I knew I had to focus my mind away from the Coronavirus pandemic and on to something more productive. I had to stop my addiction to the virus news and the daily death statistics.

Suddenly one morning, it was there. *My idea*. Perhaps it has always been there, and I have not listened closely enough. Maybe I had glossed over it. But there it was, birthed during the pandemic and ready to share with you. It is something unique, something lost and perhaps even thrilling. I realized that I had personally lived through a piece of lost Los Angeles history. I had grown up in an oil field on the beach, in Venice, California, a condition which no longer exists.

A book I admire is, *The Mirage Factory: Illusion, Imagination and the Invention of Los Angeles,* written by Gary Krist. He begins his book by pointing out that the corner of Southern California where they chose to build Los Angeles was no sensible place: "Often bone dry, lacking a natural harbor, and isolated by the rest of the country by expansive deserts and rugged mountain ranges." Early explorers passed on it, and he points out that even when Mexico did settle it in 1821, it was considered "a hinterland, a backwater without water." It was only after the Mexican-American war when Southern California became a part of the United States that anyone would come up with the wild and crazy idea of building a monster city in the desert.

Krist's book is about the "trickery" and "contrivance" which it took to bring resources, population and industry to a place that lacked them all. His story is about the extraordinary transformation from desert to the metropolis that it would become. No place in Los Angeles is more flamboyant and unexpected than Venice. That is where my story is set.

Growing Up On The Beach

I grew up on the beach in Venice, California and lived there for twenty one of my growing up years with five years out when we moved to nearby Culver City, and two years in the sorority at the University of Southern California. However, even then, most weekends were spent at the beach.

We lived in an area known today as the Marina Peninsula, now the gentrified home to Hollywood glitterati and tech geniuses. In 1945 when my three-year old self moved there with my young family, it was far different. For little-girl me it was a magical kingdom filled with endless possibility. Our front gate opened onto a narrow, seashell-filled beach, a gentle rolling surf, and easily obtained sand crabs. Next door to our cottage, limited in size due to the scarcity of building materials during World War II, was a very tall oil derrick serving the pump house which labored day and night, lulling my little sister and me to dream-filled sleep with its rhythmic whooshing sounds. Up and down it pumped.

All of that was commonplace to me. I think I have always taken that experience for granted. Now, however, looking back three quarters of a century, I have an appreciation for the fact that I have lived a piece of Los Angeles history which has completely disappeared. The oil wells have been gone for almost fifty years, the last one being capped in 1972. The marsh land where Hoppyland once stood has been transformed into a world class marina. The few houses along the ocean front that had survived the fever of oil production, have mostly given way to massive multi-million-dollar condominium buildings.

I have had the privilege of bearing witness to extraordinary land use and cultural changes in Venice across my lifetime.

Those growing up years, included living in the midst of the fourth most productive oil field in California, riding the tram on the boardwalk between the three huge amusement piers which once graced the Los Angeles coastline. The memories combined with my passion for the early history of Los Angeles and its humble beginnings, layered against the colonization of Alta California, have fueled me with creative energy and ignited my brain. Armed with this project, I know I can get through the remaining weeks, or months, of government mandated isolation. I am eager to share my story of "growing up Venice" with you.

As I tossed my thoughts of Venice history around, I shared some of them with my builder son, Dan, who has a passion for urban planning. About a day later he called me. "Mom, I have always known that you grew up on the beach, but until last night I never thought about it. I have not *processed* what that would have been like. I cannot imagine it."

Well, you can bet that Dan's reflection, "I cannot imagine it," whetted my appetite to share my experiences with you. There's something more. I recently read a line in a novel which resonates with me: "Once the storyteller is gone, so are the stories, unless they are *written down*." I have taken this to heart and written them down. The genre of this book is Narrative Non-fiction. This means that I have written the history from the perspective of the first-person narrative, sharing my stories as I remember them. Perhaps, it is a blending of my academic college-professor self with the storyteller in me.

I am hoping you enjoy it, that your imagination will catch fire as the tale unfolds. My dream is that you vicariously live some remnants of millionaire-developer Abbott Kinney's big dream of creating a Venice-of-America and appreciate all Venice's iterations across time.

I am eager for you to get a sense of what it was like to visit the old canal and collect guppies in the shadows of decaying Venetian bridges, or delight in combing the sand after a Fourth of July celebration and discovering the bounty of unlit fire crackers and sparklers!

Venice seems to keep reinventing itself, enjoying heyday after heyday. As I have discovered, it is more than Venice reinventing itself, it is about layers of dichotomous cultures living side by side in parallel universes. It is mind blowing!

Chapter One

Ever Changing Venice-of-America

*"Time is different at the beach, it moves by current, tide, and the sun,
not by clocks and calendars." Donna*

Every five or so years, my husband, Ken and I revisit one or the other's old childhood haunts. A few years back, after our fifty-year wedding anniversary get-away, we visited the church where we were married in Rolling Hills, California. It was a Sunday morning and the service had just ended. We parked the car and began strolling the grounds. The sanctuary doors were wide open. Curious, I tiptoed and looked in. It had changed so little! Almost everyone was outside sipping coffee, except for a few ladies

taking up the flowers. The pastor was folding up the satin covering for the pulpit. I knew it was okay to enter. Their friendly faces prompted me to exclaim, "Fifty years ago today we exchanged our vows right here." Needless to say, they were intrigued and wanted to hear all about it. Doing the math, the pastor hesitantly inquired, "The pastor wasn't Tom Gibson, was it?" When we answered affirmatively, the questions erupted into an enthusiastic volley. They were so excited. As the founder of their church, Reverend Gibson was a figure of great importance to them. He was before their time. We had known him well, and they hung onto each shared memory. After a bit, they offered to take our photo at the altar. It was a beautiful few minutes and our hearts were full as we returned to our car.

Recently, Ken and I were back to our old tricks of revisiting the past. This trip to my early childhood was more than a walk down Memory Lane. I had decided to write about some lost history of Los Angeles, specifically in Venice, California. This excursion was a way to stimulate my memories of the Venice of my early life.

Searching for Landmarks

We set out on a warm spring day during the global pandemic isolation orders. We packed a lunch, knowing no restaurants would be open. We planned to spend the day looking for the landmarks of my growing up years.

Ken has always been a good sport about taking me on sojourns for my writing. That church visit five years before had proven that sometimes time can stand still. However, I was keenly aware that this trip would be the polar opposite.

The hour-long trip up the 405 Freeway was a cinch as the traffic was light due to Stay-At-Home Order. We started at the famous "Venice" sign hanging across the Windward intersection. It defines the entrance to the "Venice Beach Scene." On this Tuesday in May of 2020 there were only a few people about, a rare condition. The Venice Beach of contemporary times enjoys ten million visitors a year and is the second biggest tourist draw in Southern California, surpassed only by Disneyland. The current population for the 3.17 square mile neighborhood is about 40,000. Median households earn a higher income than those of Los Angeles in general, and the population is young, with a median age of 35

The Red Car brought visitors from as far away as 50 miles. The trains unloaded at the corner of Trolley Way and Windward. Trolley Way was renamed Pacific Avenue in later years. One track ran in the middle of Venice Boulevard.

years. Venice has enjoyed a skyrocketing real estate market with seventy percent of the residents renting their homes. The last decade or so, there has been a renaissance of gentrification as big tech giants such as Google and Snap Inc. have been taking up residence. The move-in of the digital industry has earned Venice and neighboring beach cities the title "Silicon Beach." One source reports some 500 such tech and internet companies calling the West Side beach communities home.

Venice Beach is situated about 14 miles west of Los Angeles and has been an attraction since the late 1800's. My great grandparents were frequent visitors to the amusement pier at the end of the Red Car line which opened in 1894 and ran from downtown, serving Venice and Santa Monica. By 1905 Venice had separated from Ocean Park and soon claimed a population of 3000. It was attractive to Angelenos not only because of the beautiful surf and sandy beach, but also due to the amusements. Many folks were eager to escape the social controls of Los Angeles known as the "Blue Laws" which prohibited dancing and gambling. These were readily available in Venice. During Prohibition, another attraction would have been the presence of speakeasies hidden in Windward Avenue basements.

Venice is unique in the world, as a tourist attraction, but it has not always been. In the 1940's when

our family moved into the 400 square-foot house my father built in 1944, the neighborhood was industrial; part residential, part oil field, part empty lots. As the fourth largest oil field in Southern California, some four hundred and fifty oil wells hummed along, day and night during my growing up years.

As Ken slowly drove south through my old neighborhood, mostly deserted now due to the isolation orders, I thought about the rollicking, vibrant street scene for which Venice is famous. I understood that once the world reopened, normal life would return and the carnival atmosphere of this section of Venice Beach would once again come to life.

As we moved along, I scanned my memory searching for other such lively places I've encountered in my world travels. Certainly, the street artists creating chalk drawings on the sidewalk in front of the Uffizi Gallery in Florence, Italy, are noteworthy. Barcelona's Las Ramblas Street is an incredible attraction due the colorful array of performers lining the sidewalk posing as statues. For a price, one might have their photo taken with an "18th century lady," completely covered in gold spray paint, or pose in front of the "Statue of Liberty."

Grandfather R.W. Lewis, Sr. enjoying the beach c 1918

Chums posing in front of lifeguard station Venice Beach. Notice girls have written "LAHS" for Los Angeles High School – "Best." Grandmother Vera-May "Maymie" in center. Note life saving equipment.

Pier 39 in San Francisco also offers street entertainment, but like other such places in the world, it pales when compared to the elaborate goings-on at Venice Beach, which is sometimes billed as the "craziest beach in the world." There's live music, gymnastic performers, fortune tellers, jugglers, food stands, vendors, muscle and basketball competitors, and eccentric weirdness, often accompanied by the scent of potent marijuana smoke. Elaborate murals decorate many of the buildings and help define the

Our house is behind Mrs. Moore's big shake house mid screen. 1940's Venice Peninsula.

2.5 mile long pedestrian promenade. Many visitors themselves dress up in costume, adding to the incredible people watching scene. All this activity is set against a backdrop of hundreds of roller skaters, skate boarders, bicyclists and joggers. On a lucky day, a tourist might even encounter a Hollywood camera crew set up to shoot a movie scene.

Marina Peninsula

Continuing our drive south on Pacific Avenue, we crossed Washington Boulevard. A glance to my left and the building that had once been the Edgewater Market met my eye. It is a Starbucks now. Suddenly an old memory flooded into my brain. I could envision myself at about age four, walking toward the back of the store, past the butcher counter, to the refrigerated shelves which held the milk and margarine. I remember picking out the margarine. Back at home I was the lucky one who got the best job. I got to mix the yellow food coloring into the soft margarine so that it would look like yellow butter. I loved doing that. I would drag the wooden dinette chair to the kitchen sink, climb up on and carefully mix the ingredients. I felt very grown up. There was still great scarcity of goods due to WWII.

As we drove along, the neighborhood became the Venice peninsula, known now as Marina Peninsula. We passed my old elementary school, Nightingale, where I attended first through third grade. My research showed that for some years during the 1930's it was closed due to the pollution from the oil fields. The handball court and tether ball pole were gone, replaced by classrooms. It is a charter school now with a new name, and for a time it was known as Anchorage School. I remembered that in Room 3, first grade, the teacher lined the top of the blackboard with letters, big ones and little ones. It was where I learned to read. Three times a week an older student would come and get me and take me to speech therapy. At recess, our class would go to the cafeteria to buy a snack. For a dime I could buy hot chocolate and a graham cracker. I made friends with a girl named Julie Ann Niece. She lived in the canals. Sometimes her clothes were torn and dirty. She never had money for snack. My dad would give me enough money so that I could buy Julie Ann a hot chocolate and a graham cracker. She was a pretty girl with freckles on her nose. I decided that if I ever had a daughter I would name her Julie, as I did.

The next year when my little sister, Jackie, was old enough for kindergarten, I would wait at the gate for her to get out of school. The two of us would walk to the corner in front of Edgewater Market where I would take Jackie's hand. We would look both ways and walk across Washington to the corner. Still holding her hand, we would very carefully cross Pacific. Once we got to the boardwalk it was

Nightingale Elementary, later Anchorage School. The smaller building in the right front was the cafeteria and kindergarten where Jackie went to class. The cocoa and graham crackers were in that cafeteria. Looking up and south about five blocks would be where our house was.

smooth sailing. No more streets to cross. We were headed to the playground where our mom worked. She had a network of local shopkeepers who acted as lookouts for her. They checked on us as our two little blonde heads passed by. Everyone called out to us and waved. George was our favorite. He worked in the diner directly across the walk from the playground. He wore a white cap and cooked delicious hamburgers. Our mom still laughs when she talks about her "network of spies" looking out for her girls.

Ken and I proceeded south a few more blocks when I spotted one of the old canal bridges. My stomach did a flip. Three such dilapidated canal bridges existed in the 1940's when the waterway was known as the Venice Canal. The bridges had been closed with chains across their opening and warning signs to keep out. I felt a bit breathless as I realized that this bridge had been restored and was in use. My excitement grew. I was prepared for my past landmarks to be eradicated. I certainly did not expect to have some aspect preserved! I hope I was not bouncing in my seat. Ken eased the car to a curb parking spot. I jumped out with camera in hand.

I crossed the empty street and rushed to the bridge . Sweet old memories reminded me that this spot once marked our favorite guppy collecting place in the murky waters of the canal. A sign at the entrance of the bridge declared: *Ballona Lagoon – Marine Preserve Public Access Trail.* I was so excited!! I had not expected this! I marveled that it had been returned to its 1905 glory.

My mind's eye recalled my little-girl-self stooping over the water with my fish net in hand. We loved catching guppies. This activity, however, required supervision as we had to cross the busy street, and the water was deep. Our dad was happy to join in. We were quick with our nets and always caught a few of the tiny creatures. We would carry them home in jelly jars and place them in our bigger aquarium where we could watch them grow. It was a big project, holding our interest for some time, as it required us to change their brackish water. Eventually, we would return them to the lagoon.

I took some photos. We continued our tour. Across the canal, facing the water, is a row of multi-million-dollar homes. They are beautiful. I wondered if their owners were aware that once upon a time in the early 1950's, little kids like me met Hopalong Cassidy there, on the land under their houses?

Many of the homes have been built upon the former site of actor William Boyd's Hoppyland. I am guessing they have no idea. In fact, they probably don't even know the famous TV cowboy, Hoppy. They may not even care. I grinned to myself as if I had a secret. I wonder if that's why history appeals to me so much. The more one studies, the more intriguing secrets are revealed.

Canal Bridge - guppy hunting

Marina del Rey Channel

As we came to the dead-end of Pacific Avenue, Ken pulled into a parking space. Our car faced the ocean entrance to the Marina del Rey harbor. We parked and got out. When I was a girl there was no marina. It was possible to walk south on the beach from our home all the way to Manhattan Beach. The ocean only flowed through Ballona Creek where there was a bridge connecting Venice to Playa del Rey. As we stood on the jetty looking south, I could see the old Ballona Creek bridge, still arching across Ballona Creek. I always loved that bridge. It was a good fishing spot. I thought we might need another research "trip" which would include walking on that old bridge.

Ken remembered fishing for croakers on it with his father, and when he was older, riding the big surfing waves that streamed into the channel. His friends would follow and pick him up in their outboard boat. Ken loved to share those Ballona Creek surf stories. Now there is a wide breakwater spanning across both channel entrances. No surf today, probably no more big waves coming through at all.

I remembered a day when I was in my early teens when I took off walking on the wet sand. It felt so good that I kept going. I crossed the Ballona Creek bridge and walked all the way to the Hyperion power plant in Manhattan Beach. It was probably six miles each way. That long walk gave me a sense of power; that I could go anywhere on my own. Today such a walk is impossible due to the opening of the marina.

Marina del Rey Channel

Ken and I walked out on the jetty. The water was red with the bioluminescence that had been present the past few weeks in Southern California. The smell was strong. It stank! I'd had enough, and we turned back toward the car when I noticed that the house at the beginning of the beach strand was one I had always known. I felt like I had run into an old friend. It is a big black shake sided two-story. It, with a few other luxurious old-timer homes are still standing. They are reminders of the grandeur that had once been the oceanfront, left behind from the turn of the 20th century when Venice was known as Venice-of-America. This house was probably constructed between 1906-1911.

Discovering Landmarks

We climbed back into the car. Ken kept a slow pace as he turned north on the Speedway. There were no cars about. Our slow pace was not a problem. I searched out the street numbers. Almost all of the markers for my memory have vanished. Even the streets have been renamed. I was looking for the 4400 block, the site of our house at 4411 Ocean Front Walk. I knew it would be hard to find. Mrs. Moore's big brown shake 1900's house, next door to ours on the south side, was long gone. The other

neighbor, the big oil well, had been dismantled in the late 50's. Even the beach itself was so different. Though the address is Ocean Front Walk, there never was a walk. When we opened our front yard gate in the 1940's there was only soft white sand at this southern peninsula of Venice Beach.

I kept a look-out for the correct site as more memories crowded my mind. Our house had been situated close to the street so that the front yard would be available for some future room addition. My little sister, Jackie, and I had our own pup tent set up in the front yard. I have included a photo taken by my father from high in the oil derrick, looking down at our house and the neighborhood. If you look closely, the pup tent is in the far right of the photo. We loved the tent because it offered privacy from our parents' eyes. It was a place where we could eat all the candy bars our grandfather would

Apartment Building in Alley. Circa 1920's. photo 2020.

have given us from his pharmacy. In fact, the entire sandy floor of the pup tent was covered in candy wrappers. We liked it like that, though I now realize it was evidence of our candy eating had prying eyes looked in our tent.

Finally we found 4400. We stopped. Ken pulled to the side of the street so I could get out. A massive condominium building covered what had been our lot, plus the lot where Mrs. Moore's house sat, and the one south of it.

Though the houses I knew were gone, I looked across the Speedway to the alley behind what would have been our house. I crossed the narrow Speedway and walked into the alley. What a find! Some parts of the past remained. A big two-story stucco apartment building still stood, a landmark from my past. I walked further into the alley. I remembered the big family, the Persingers who lived on the right side. There had been very few children nearby, no doubt due to the plethora of oil wells, and the economic scarcities of war-time America.

Jackie and I were grateful to know the Persinger kids. They were our playmates. We formed sort of a roving gang of four to six-year-olds, prowling the neighborhood. The girl I liked the best was named Jannie. Jackie recalls how much she enjoyed Jannie's family's outdoor shower. She remembers rinsing off after we had been in the ocean, warming up in their shower. I recalled us playing kick ball and tag with Jannie and her siblings. At dusk you could hear us calling out, *Ollie Ollie Oxen Free Free Free!* Finally, our parents would call us in.

I crossed back and made my way to the beach front of the building. I stood exactly where our front gate had once opened and faced the ocean. A soft breeze rustled my hair and I smiled. This part of Venice has always been pretty quiet, even when it was an oil field. I stared out to the surf line. It was so far away, perhaps 300 yards. The county had extended it when I was in my teens. A huge brown pipe had bisected the beach for a many years, pouring hundreds of thousands of tons of sand dredged from the nearby wetlands onto the beach.

I took a minute to imagine us as children playing in the sand. I let the memories in and could visualize my mom in front of us as we combed the beach searching for shells. It was such a different beach. It was shallow with the waves breaking about twenty feet from the front gate. We would be collecting treasures. Our mom prized the moon stones and the sea glass. Our collections grew across the years.

Our little kid gang collected sand dollars, snails and shells. We constructed rock and seaweed villages and made-believe that the snail shells were people. We built sandcastles and hid from each other. We combed the beach for treasure. The best finds came after windstorms when the sand betrayed the treasure beneath. Mostly, we found pennies and bottle caps, but once we found a diamond ring. We gave it to our mom. She was pretty sure that it was costume jewelry. When we were a bit older, we would collect soda bottles and turn them into Tony's Market at the corner of Washington and Speedway. Our eyes would light up when Tony, the owner, [Nick's Market now] handed over pennies and sometimes a nickel!

View from front of 4411 - wide beach extended in 1950's

"Toot Toot! Here comes the Helms Man!"

Another particularly stunning economic event was heralded by the loud "toot toot" whistle of the Helms Bakery truck. Jackie remembers that with that loud whistle we would come running, "We would have money for a donut and we climbed WAY up and stood on the floor of the truck. Then the man opened many of the huge flat drawers for us to make our selection. Great aromas and fun!" My memories were of standing at the back of the truck while the smooth wooden drawers were pulled out revealing the chocolate éclairs and cream puffs. I always admired the silver change maker attached to our Helm's Man's belt. He came by every week day. We also enjoyed the delights of the little yellow and blue truck, when it came by at our grandparents' house in Hollywood. The Helms Man was a childhood highlight.

Paul Helms, retire banker turned baker, opened his bakery on Venice Boulevard between Washington Boulevard near Culver City in 1931. He began with 11 delivery coaches and 32 employees. By the next year he had become the official baker for the 1932 Olympics. The motto was "daily at your door." The Helms trucks could be found traveling routes as far north as Fresno and as far into Laguna Niguel in Orange County to the south.

Even though the breads and pastries were never sold in the supermarket, the Helms business plan

prospered until 1969. Millions of Southern Californians looked forward to that "toot toot." It did not hurt that a visit to the factory was the standard third grade field trip for students in the Los Angeles Unified School District. I remember my third grade trip. I stood next to a huge vat of dough being kneaded by a large metal paddle. Today the big Helms factory building is a retail furniture design center and restaurants. It's a popular meeting spot where people can gather.

Donna at Helms – June 2020

Firecrackers

A favorite growing up time was the day after the 4th of July. We would comb the beach for sparklers which had not been used; sometimes there'd be a firecracker or a rocket. One summer I found a firecracker. I kept it to myself until it was dark. It was my job to take the trash out to burn in the incinerator which was right next to the Speedway. As I lit the fire, I had the idea to take the firecracker out of my pocket. I can almost see myself now. I held the fuse of the firecracker out. I carefully struck the match and lit it. However, I failed to toss it. It went off in my hand. It was so loud that my ears rang the entire rest of the evening. I scared myself. With the flash of its explosion, I realized I could have blinded myself. That was such a dumb move that I never did tell anyone. In fact, revealing it now, is the first I have ever confessed it. Ever.

In thinking about the band of us little kids wandering free, doing as we pleased, it seems so odd to me now. My grandchildren have always been heavily supervised. Even now, our youngest at ten-years old, Caroline, is carefully watched over. None of us would consider allowing her to walk, unescorted, the half mile home from her elementary school. In fact, someone picks her up each day. Back then, we were allowed to explore. Even my own children in the early 70's, in San Juan Capistrano, spent most of their free time outside exploring the creek beds and catching yellow racer snakes. It's interesting to think about. I am not sure why. I don't know if child abductions are more frequent now. Certainly, the news is more instant and perhaps more scary. Youth today seem to live a more indoor, sheltered life. In discussing this with friends, so many people quickly offered that when they were kids, "we had to be in when the street lights turned on."

Sometimes when the Persinger kids weren't at home, when it was just Jackie and me, we would visit an older girl, Wanda, who was a shut-in. Wanda

Donna and Jackie playing in the front yard c. 1946

was born a "blue baby" which held great mystery to us. We understood that she had something wrong with her heart and that attending school would be too dangerous for her. She was an only child, homeschooled by, what seemed to us, to be very old parents. She had a huge collection of dolls. We would while away entire afternoons in her room playing with those beautiful dolls. Even now, seventy years later, I can recall the musty smell of her home and feel its too-warm temperature. Her family guarded her health. Many times we would stop by and her mother would turn us away, saying that Wanda was not well.

Years later, after we had grown up and moved away, I encountered her in the library at Santa Monica College. We had greeted one another warmly. I was pleased to see that she had come to have what seemed to me, a normal life. I guess even back then as a seven-year old, I could see that she missed out on playing outside with us. I think that I must have worried about her.

One cold winter day, Jackie and I were on our own. We were too young for school and were looking for entertainment. We were hiding behind a sand dune next to the Speedway. It's hard to admit that we had the idea of throwing pebbles at the cars as they sped by. I was the oldest. I think it was my idea. You can imagine our horror when one of the cars stopped. An angry man stomped over to where we were ducking down behind the sand dune and told us that he was taking us to jail! We were mortified. *Jail!!* We had no idea that it was not a practice for a stranger to take children to jail. With big round eyes and our hearts pounding, we promised never again to throw rocks at the cars. With that agreement, and probably seeing the terror on our faces, he let us off with just the warning. Truly he scared us straight. We never threw pebbles again!

The Grunion are Running!

As I squinted to see the surf line, I thought about the nights when the grunion were running. Catching grunion was another highlight of my childhood! The slippery little fish are a species that spawn on the beaches in the night during the spring and summer. It was a grand adventure! It did not happen often, and we never tired of it. We would wait until dark, often we had already gone to sleep. Our dad would wake us up and whisper, "The grunion are running!" We would scramble to get out on the beach. The contest was to see who could catch the most grunion and wrestle them into the pails. It was very exciting as hundreds of the slippery little silver fish would wash across our feet and slip out of our hands. We would be laughing and yelling with delight. Sometimes others would join us at the surf line, neighbors or people who drove to the shore for the event. The little sardine-like fish were supposedly good to eat when they were fried. We never ate them, we just threw them back. The joy was in the catching!

I pulled my thoughts back to the present and returned to the car. We had many more stops to make. I wanted to think more about all this, particularly the changes to the way people have chosen to utilize the precious beach land. Today the peninsula area is a glamorous high-end residential district, but 70 years ago it was a significant commercial petroleum field. In the late 1800's, the nearby boardwalk was a place of amusement with a casino and attractions for the children. By early 1900 the tobacco millionaire, Abbot Kinney began the construction for his Venice-of-America. Earlier still, before the Spanish colonist arrived, it was home to the Chumash People, then the Tongva People. I had a lot to think about.

Heading Home

After more hours of walking the empty boardwalk and regaling Ken with tales from the past, we settled into quiet and headed home to San Juan Capistrano. As we sped south down the 405 Freeway, I was surprised to discover that after all these years together, we still have so much to say to one another. I also knew there would be many more days of global isolation, and that I would have plenty of time to share with you, all that I wanted you to know about some lost pieces of Los Angeles history.

Donna cartwheel practice

Deserted Venice Beach -homeless camping on sand

Donna and Ken have Venice Beach to themselves. May 2020

Looking north toward 4411 Ocean Front Walk

Chapter Two

The Heydays at the Beach

"If you are lucky enough to live by the sea, you are lucky enough." Unknown

A few days after our research trip to discover what remained of *my* Venice, I began sifting through our family's old beach photos. My great grandparents, Charles and Lydia Lewis, intrigue me. In their photos, they are dressed in formal 19th century attire sitting sweetly together. It seems an odd contrast to see their style of seaside clothing, so unlike today's scanty bathing suits. In one photo my great grandparents are posed in front of a Penny Arcade sign. In another, dated 1900, they are sitting on the sand. I am certain that they were enjoying the ocean front amusements for which Abbot Kinney would become famous.

My family, my paternal great grandparents on both sides, arrived in Los Angeles in the late 1880's when the train came through from the East. Charles and Lydia were living in Des Moines, Iowa when counted for the census of 1885. Their son, my grandfather, Ray Lewis, was in the first grade at Los Angeles School in 1890.

Charles and Lydia Lewis – A day at the beach 1900

R. W. Lewis Drug Company on West Washington Boulevard

R. W. Lewis Sr.

My big box of old photographs reveals a lot of beach-side enthusiasm on the part of our long-ago relations. After the turn of the 20th Century, in 1905, Abbot Kinney would rise to fame as the architect of Venice-of-America, and ultimately, almost a century later, would continue to be celebrated for his genius. In 1990, Los Angeles City officials renamed West Washington Boulevard to Abbott Kinney Boulevard. Recently, it has become something of an "in" spot.

In the 1950's my grandfather moved his last pharmacy to that street. During the

previous fifteen years, he operated his R. W. Lewis Drug Company from the corner of Sunset Boulevard and Gardner in Hollywood. It was a glittering store with a sparkling medicine ball hanging from the ceiling above the door. It had a long soda fountain lining the west wall of the store. I loved it. Jackie and I would spin on the wooden stools waiting for our chocolate malts to be made. It was a fantasy world filled with malted milk balls, comics, candy, and sodas.

I was older for this Venice store. I spent many afternoons stocking shelves at the R. W. Lewis Drug Company at 1358 West Washington Boulevard. It was an ordinary neighborhood business district. In the 40's and 50's it was by no means a "hot spot." The storefront is still there. It is a high-end dress shop now.

1358 Abbot Kinney - Store front in 2020

Abbot Kinney's Vision

Had Abbot Kinney not actualized his vision of creating a mythical town, my grandparents probably would not have bought a vacant lot at 4411 Ocean Front Walk in the early 1940's. My father would not have built a cottage on it, and I would not be telling this story. Kinney had enough gravitas to pull off an extraordinary venture. He possessed adequate political capital to have the southern section of Ocean Park renamed Venice, enough juice to advocate for incorporation, and deep enough pockets to get it done. It's amazing, really.

Venice Pier

By the time my sister and I were five and six and a half years-old, our mother had secured a position as playground leader at the Venice Playground. The playground was situated on the sand next to the boardwalk at Windward Avenue next to the skeleton of what had once been Abbot Kinney's famous

Venice Pier

Venice Pier. My most vivid encounter with anything Abbot Kinney was the day in which my sister and I could have been killed. Once a crowd pleasing spectacle, the boarded-up pier was, by the late 40's, a dangerous blight on the coast. It was a burned out relic of its former glorious self. Only the hulking ruins stood perched high above the playground on wobbly pilings.

The playground was perhaps 75 feet south of it. On a certain day, an older girl with a tiny dog in her arms was playing on the swings with us. She dared my little sister, Jackie, and me to go out onto the boarded-up pier. She might have been nine. I think the two of us were flattered to have an older child to play with.

"C'mon let's go." She urged.

"We're not supposed to leave the playground." I responded in a worried voice.

"We'll just be gone for a few minutes!" She cajoled. "Your mom won't even know you're gone. She's busy with that carom tournament. Come on!"

That big girl kept her demands up until Jackie and I agreed to go, but *just to look*.

We sneaked up the ramp to the pier and slid in between two loose boards. We passed around the *Do Not Enter* sign and carefully made our way out onto the pier. We were far enough out that we could look down between the floorboards and see the waves crashing below. It was dark below and a little spooky. The surf was loud as it moved back and forth against the burned-out black pilings.

We scampered out a little further and climbed into some kind of old structure, maybe it was the old

Playground Venice Beach

fun house. The waves below kept rolling in and out. Suddenly, the older girl dashed across a single plank stretched precariously over a wide-open space. I remember that when she got to the other side, her little dog was shivering with fear. I looked down. It was a long way into the dark waters below.

"Come on Donna. Come on!" She taunted, "Are you chicken? Yellow chicken! Yellow Chicken!" She was goading me in a sing-song voice. She kept up the "yellow chicken" thing a few more times.

"No! It's too dangerous!" I yelled across the space. "What if we fall?" I studied the long drop underneath us.

"*Fall?* You won't fall. I did it. I'm safe. I'm not a *yellow* chicken!"

I remember that time seemed to stand still. I turned to my little sister. "Stay back!" I warned in a threatening voice. "This is scary. *Stay back*!"

With that, I quickly scooted across the plank. My heart was pounding, my checks were on fire. The girl's little dog continued to shiver. Once across, breathing hard, I squeaked, "How're we getting back?"

I looked across the chasm at Jackie who seemed to be considering joining us. "Jackie stay there!" I screamed. "I'm coming back." With that I quickly bolted across the plank, grabbed my little sister by the hand, and raced out of the condemned structure, through the space in the boards, down the rough wooden ramp. Without looking back, we made it quickly across the distance to the playground.

Jackie looked at me with big round, scared eyes. My heart was thudding almost out of my chest. I imagined what could have happened had I fallen. What if Jackie had followed me across? She was so little…

We sat in a corner of the sand box for a long time. Later, our mom came looking for us. We never told her about our terrible adventure. It was our dangerous little secret. I'll never forget that day. It was my last visit to that pier. A few years later, it was completely dismantled. Today there is absolutely no sign that it was ever there. No sign of the risky business of two little girls.

Perhaps you would be interested to know something more about the Venice-of-America genius Abbot Kinney. I've had plenty of time to research as California has entered its ninth week of mandated lockdown due to the pandemic. We are not supposed to leave our homes except to exercise.

Abbot Kinney - The Dreamer

Abbot Kinney was a man with a heart and a sense of the bigger picture. He left California better for having lived here. History books describe him as a "utopian visionary," a "conservationist" and a "staunch advocate for Native American rights."

One of my deep interests is California history. When I became a Mission San Juan Capistrano docent four years ago, I was presented with the opportunity to teach California history to fourth graders. It's a delightful volunteer job, as some 50,000 or so students visit us at the Mission each year. With that in mind, I was particularly fascinated to learn that Kinney had a concern for the Native people. As a younger man he had spent time on a Sioux Indian Reservation in the Dakota Territory mapping the reservation as part of a United States Geological Team. In 1882 he served as co-agent and interpreter to author, activist Helen Hunt Jackson who was exposing the deplorable condition of the Native Americans at the missions. In 1883 Kinney and Jackson co-authored a 56-page paper on those conditions, calling for government relief. Their actions resulted in the Mission Indian Act of 1891. That led to the establishment of an agency to create better conditions for the Native Americans.

Kinney was also passionate about conservation. As Chairman of the California State Board of Forestry, he developed an agency to protect the forests of the San Gabriel Mountains from the routine burnings by ranchers who wanted more cattle grazing pastures. He brought eucalyptus trees to California and with his pal, naturalist John Muir, he established the forerunner of the Angeles National Forest. He and Muir also did the legwork for establishment of Yosemite National Park.

Beautiful c. 1900's Homes

Kinney's Early Life

Kinney was born in 1850 in New Jersey to well-off, upper middle class parents. Tall for his age, 6'2" by age 16, he was good with languages and had the opportunity to travel aboard for much of his education. He was fluent in seven languages. By the age of 24 years he was made junior partner in his older brother's tobacco business. He became a buyer for the Kinney Brothers Tobacco business out of New York City. This afforded him more opportunity for world travel. In 1890 the Kinney Brothers' tobacco company was bought up by the American Tobacco Company, which held a near monopoly on the cigarette market. The brothers received $5 million in stock shares, further increasing their wealth.

Later, Kinney sold his shares to his brother and invested in Southern California real estate developments.

It was ultimately Southern California's dry climate which inspired Kinney to stay. A lifetime asthmatic, when he finally got a dose of the dry SoCal air, he was sold. He bought up some 550 acres in the San Gabriel Mountains above Pasadena and built Kinneola, a beautiful mountain property where he constructed a spectacular home, cultivated gardens, and raised citrus. He married Margaret Thornton, daughter of a California Supreme Court Justice, and together they welcomed five children. The heat of the Sierra Madre summers was unpleasant for Margaret, so they built a vacation home in Santa Monica.

In 1891 Kinney and his partner, Francis Ryan, turned their development attention to the beach area south of Santa Monica known as Ocean Park. They purchased a controlling interest in a casino which housed a restaurant and amusements. The quest for land continued and they purchased a large portion of the Rancho La Ballona which extended along the beach from southern Santa Monica to Ballona Creek. They began an enthusiastic development of the mile and a half tract of land along the Santa Monica-Ocean Park corridor. They created a golf course, a horse-racing track and a boardwalk. They sold housing lots, built parks, and piers. The Ocean Park area blossomed to life. Private citizens built beautiful Victorian-style homes on the pedestrian streets which lined the boardwalk. Some of those homes are still standing in 2020.

Venice-of-America

Kinney and Ryan were laser-focused on their successful Ocean Park development when Ryan suddenly died in 1898. Ryan's widow sold her shares to developers whose ideas were not in sync with Kinney's. In a famous flip of a coin, the men decided to split the property and go their separate ways. The desirable property was clearly the northern section, a bit north of Venice including Ocean Park. The southern section was mostly wetlands where the Los Angeles River fed into Ballona Creek and flowed to the ocean. Kinney chose the swampy marshland and began to fulfill his most elaborate scheme yet!

He envisioned a magical resort reminiscent of Venice, Italy. No doubt his world travels and his visit to the Chicago World's Fair in 1893 influenced his vision. The 1893 World's Fair was a big deal celebrating 400 years since Columbus

Abbot Kinney - Genius Dreamer

discovered America. Its centerpiece was a lake, representative of Columbus' journey across the sea. The lake, in combination with the fair's promotion of "city beautiful" features, triggered Kinney's imagination. Like so many creative people, I'm guessing that the "city beautiful" possibilities lay dormant in his mind, waiting for just the right moment to burst forth.

With the toss of that coin, tails, he was in a position to make his dream a reality. By 1904 he began construction in the swampland. He was developing a world class beach paradise which would be known as Venice-of-America. It would boast seven canals, a large saltwater lagoon, a pier, an auditorium, a bathhouse, an amphitheater, a ship restaurant-hotel, a dance pavilion, a heated saltwater swimming pool, a working miniature railroad, and more.

Teams of mules were dispatched to excavate the marsh area south of Windward to create canals and a large lagoon. Kinney established a grand opening deadline. The digging went too slowly for him to meet that date. A man of action, Kinney brought in steam shovels to speed up the work.

He experienced major setbacks. The most damaging problem was a disastrous winter storm which hit in March before his planned July 4th, 1905 grand opening. That storm destroyed the pier, leaving a debris field of pilings washed up on the beach. Even with that, he was determined to meet that opening date. Kinney brought in 600 more workers and got the job done. Venice-of-America opened July 4, 1905 to a crowd of 40,000 eager Angelenos.

The population for the City of Los Angeles in 1900 was just over 100,000. Based upon the enthusiastic beach photos in our family stash, I think my great grandparents and my great aunt would

Digging Canals 1904 –Courtesy LA Public Library

have been a part of that opening day crowd. My great aunt Fay, a socialite known as "Hats" due to her profusion of fancy headwear, was a whirlwind of energy. There's no way, at age 25 years, she would have missed an occasion as enticing as the opening of a new city. She would have dragged my grandfather, a shy 21-year-old along.

Opening day offered an exhilarating program: concerts featuring 400 voices supported by the 42-piece Venice-of-America Band, art exhibits, swim races, diving exhibitions, dancing contests, and a fireworks display over the lagoon in the evening. On top of all that, it was a great opportunity for the wealthy to purchase property. Prospective buyers of the canal lots, for example, were loaded onto the miniature electric train and chauffeured around a three-mile track. It is said that $405,000 dollars' worth of property was sold that day. (Alexander, p. 19)

Kinney's concept for moving visitors about Venice-of-America was to provide choices as they arrived by streetcar from downtown. They could stroll the footpaths, float in a gondola serenaded by a gondolier, or enjoy a miniature train ride.

Crowds Clamor to the Piers

The tourist postcards show a dazzling array of entertainment possibilities, however a year into it, Kinney discovered that his rather high-brow concerts and lectures were not drawing in the masses he had hoped for. In 1906, aiming to attract more patrons, he arranged to bring in thrills as attractions. This new plan included creation of a Midway with rides that had proven themselves at the Chicago's World's Fair, and at Portland's Lewis and Clark Centennial Exhibition. These additional crowd pleasers assured greater attendance. The beach area throngs swelled to some 350,000 on summer weekends, as families swarmed to the piers and activities.

My family was included in the gatherings. There is a photo of my grandmother, Vera May Lewis, "Maymie," sitting on a mule with a mural of the Venice Pier in the background. She was born in 1901 in plenty of time to enjoy the glory years of Venice-of-America. I think she is about five years-old in the picture. There are many photos of her as she grew up at the beach with her "chums." Her favorite ride was the fast-moving Dragon Slide. Participants sat on burlap bags and thrilled to the long, exciting ride.

I found these Venice-of-America postcards and others in her papers. She kept these across her long life. Clearly, she treasured them. They were published by Rieder in Los Angeles but made in Germany. (The color rotogravure process was in Germany. My husband, Ken's grandfather Emil, brought it to America from Germany about 1915).

Great Grandparents enjoying Venice in it's heyday c. 1900

Grandeur of Attractions

I'm sorry to have missed the glory days of Venice, but thankfully historians have left us a record. Carolyn Alexander's black and white book, *Images of Venice,* (1999), offers wonderful details about the specifics on the pier. If you are interested, I urge you to read it. The captions below are from a page of her photo history. They allow a peep into the world of Venice-of-America.

Here are some of the captions below old photos of the Midway on the pier from her book. The Midway was named "Midway Plaisance." The photo shows "*a bevy of odd buildings and even stranger performers:" The streets of Cairo [Egyptian exhibit], Darkness and Dawn [fun house], Temple of Mirth [fun house], Madame Fatima [belly dancer], The Igorots [Filipino headhunters], and Bosco Eats Them Alive [reptiles] were among the features.*"

Other photos in Alexander's book show water performances, band concerts performed twice daily, swimming races, a trained wild animal exhibition, an oriental exhibition, and children's dancing lessons. The rides were elaborate as well*: "Race through the Clouds" was east of the Lagoon attracting big crowds while the Giant Dipper at the end of the pier offered more thrills. Patrons could ride ninety-nine feet through a dragon's belly on a burlap bag in the Dragon Slide, and afterward visit Alber's Waffle parlor or enjoy goodies in the Chocolate Garden in the Ballroom."*

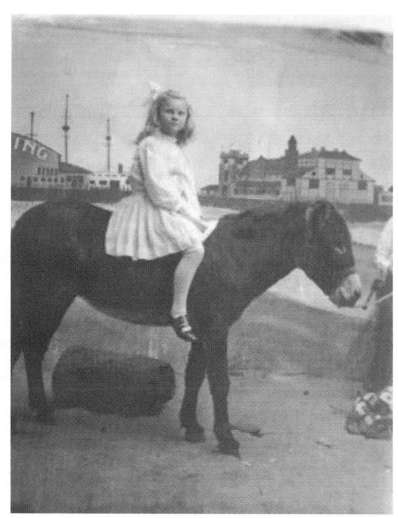

Maymie aged 5 Venice

Elephants in Venice-of-America

One photo shows a herd of large elephants standing on one of the arched bridges on the Grand Canal. It was a publicity stunt. Kinney encouraged the circus to winter in his Venice-of-America, which it did for many years. Kinney liked to play Santa to the local children at the lavish Christmas parties he hosted. I read a quote by him where he declared that he'd rather have "too many gifts for the children than disappoint even one child." He also brought in headliners like Suffragette, Susan B. Anthony and Evangelist, Aimee Semple McPherson, to fill his auditorium.

Hotels and restaurants were built in the area to accommodate the crowds of tourists. Our grandmother, Maymie, is pictured in front of the Cadillac Hotel built in 1914 at the corner of Ocean Front Walk and Dudley Street. It is still standing.

Overflow crowds were accommodated in two hundred and fifty canvas cottages known as Villa City. They were constructed along one of the canals. A story in Delores Hanney's *The Lure of the Sea*, describes the experience of summering in one of those tents. Even though they were a more economical way to enjoy the resort, the author of the essay described tent living as "opulent."

The boardwalk was a crowded place, filled with the delicious smells of freshly baked cookies and other goodies. Merchant stalls lined the sides of the walkway. In 1920 electric trams were brought in. They transported tourists back and forth between the piers. The trams were still running when my sister and I visited the piers as little girls to see our grandfather.

Maymie c 1914 – Cadillac Hotel building still standing in 2020

Maymie c. 1927 (our father behind her)

Automobiles Bring Change

To say that Abbot Kinney's experiment was a raving success would be an understatement, however it was not to persevere exactly as he had masterminded it. How could he foresee the dominance of the automobile? How could he have envisioned a time when his beautiful system of canals would be paved over to make way for Henry Ford's "machines?"

In 1908 Henry Ford turned out his Model T car and sold 1700 of them to the rich as novelties. By 1910 there were some 8000 of them on the roads across America with only 144 miles of pavement. Between 1908 and 1927, an astonishing 15 million Model T's would take to the roads and pavement would follow.

g on the Canals, Venice, Cal.

Kinney died in 1920. A month later a fire devastated the pier. His son, Thornton, was then in charge. The pier was gone. Unfortunately in a move to preserve his estate for his heirs, Kinney's Will specified that no funds could be withdrawn for a period of ten years. He did not foresee a tragedy such as the fire. History shows that Thornton had to hustle to get the support and money needed to rebuild the

Tent City - Oskar Newman Post Card c. 1915

pier. He managed to obtain funds based upon his family's reputation.

He rebuilt and the crowds kept coming. Over the next few years, however, taxes began to mount. Bills kept rolling in. The worst problem lay with the canals. Silt began to fill them, plus they were subject to flooding and pollution. To complicate things, automobiles became so popular that the tourists began to arrive in them. Both parking and street access were limited. Venetians looked to their powerful neighbor, Los Angeles, for help. The Venice City Council recognized the problem and discussed solutions.

In 1926 the City of Venice made an agreement with Los Angeles to be annexed. The City Council of Los Angeles wasted no time. Before too many years, the city filled in the canals and paved them over. Streets were needed to accommodate beachgoers. The former romantic lagoon became a rather odd, overly large, traffic circle at the foot of Windward Avenue. It remains today.

Story of Venice Mural at the Post Office

In 1939, as part of the New Deal, the U. S. Treasury Department funded a post office on the traffic circle. The post office's signature piece was a spectacular 10' x 20' mural painted on canvas by well-respected artist, Edward Biberman. The mural depicts Kinney in the foreground surrounded by scenes of Venice. Looking at the depiction, the left side has glamorous beach scenes, showing sunbathers, children at play in the sand, and a flirtatious sailor with a young lady. There are checker players under the shade of a portico set against the rides on the pier. The purple dragon ride and the ship restaurant are shown. The rollercoaster and lagoons are the background to Kinney's image in the Biberman mural. On the right side is a scene of industrial Venice complete with oil derricks, workers, and businessmen considering the oil wells.

The mural was a fixture in my growing up Venice years. Each time I had post office business, Abbott Kinney's face looked down on me from high on the wall. As a young person, I didn't pay much attention to it. Across my growing up years, I was unaware of Abbot Kinney's name, but I knew the mural.

When the United States Post Service decided to move out of the Venice branch in 2011, there was a *Save the Post Office* campaign. Venice residents felt strongly about preserving the historic building and making it available to the public. It was purchased by preservationist and big-time movie producer, Joel Silver of *Lethal Weapon* and *Die Hard* fame. Silver has repurposed the historic building into offices and a screening room for his production company. He signed a covenant that he and his successors, would

Venice Post Office Biberman Mural – Public Domain

41

preserve the building, and artist Edward Biberman's "Story of Venice" mural. He promised some public access.

Recent newspaper coverage seems positive; implying that the citizens of Venice can trust Joel Silver to be a man of his word. His detractors are less enthusiastic and think that the building should have been converted to a public use. On the day in which Ken and I visited the old post office, everything was shut down and fenced due to the pandemic closures. We did not try to gain access.

The End of an Era

Even with most of the canals paved over, the arrival of the Great Depression in 1929, and the discovery of oil, the crowds continued to come to the pier amusements. Visitors enjoyed the Venice Pier, the walk along the boardwalk to the Ocean Park Pier, and the charming colonnades along Windward Avenue. As the worsening economy affected patrons, new rides and attractions were introduced to draw them in. Gambling having been banned, the game of Bingo was conceived in such a way that it was legal gambling. As Prohibition gained a strong foothold, speakeasies proliferated in the basements of the buildings on Windward Avenue. Bands and dancing became popular.

During the scarcity of the war years, 24-hour marathon dancing became a competitive spectator

sport. Events such as beauty contests, muscle building exhibitions, and various kinds of races were highly publicized. The goal was to keep people coming to Venice.

Once peace was declared in May of 1945, the soldiers, newly relieved of their duties, found joy at the pier. The Kinney family believed the future to be bright. They believed that peace time would bring prosperity when the pier amusements would again be king.

We can only imagine the shock to the Kinney family, when in 1946 the City of Los Angeles refused to renew the Kinney Company lease on the tidelands. As Alexander put it, "the Kinney family was outraged. The whole of Venice had belonged to their father, and only through his generosity did the city now own the land." My guess is that he granted ownership of the canals to the City of Venice.

The City of Los Angeles ordered the Venice Pier to be torn down. Soon after, another horrendous fire raced through it, turning it to ruin. The pier I remember is the burned-out hulk waiting to be torn down. It was ordered closed in 1946, but the last remains were not dismantled until about 1952. This is part of the reason I wanted to share this story with you. The ten million visitors each year to the scene at the beach at Windward Avenue are probably oblivious to the magnificence of that magical pier. I can still imagine it because its cousin up the boardwalk, the Ocean Park Pier, was alive and well, booming actually, across my childhood. Of course it too is long gone.

While I never knew the Venice Pier at the height of its attractiveness, I got to experience the Ocean Park Pier built to the north just up the boardwalk. It was a significant landmark until its final demise in the winter of 1975.

BATH HOUSE AND BEACH, OCEAN PARK

Western Publishing - Vera May Lewis collection

Chapter Three

The Magic of Ocean Park Pier in the 1940's

When I was a child three piers stood between Venice and Santa Monica: the relic of Venice Pier, the exciting Ocean Park Pier, and the more *boring* Santa Monica Pier. My Venice Pier visits were on my father's shoulders. I was too young to keep them in my memory, but I was not too young to remember my childhood adventures on the Ocean Park Pier, not to be confused with the later version, the glamorous and highly publicized Pacific Ocean Park pier of 1958, known by us locals as P.O.P. The Ocean Park Pier, its early iteration, stands out in my memory as one of the very most wonderful places I have ever known.

CROWDS IN FRONT OF BATH HOUSE, OCEAN PARK

Donna and Jackie were devotees to all the fun this Ocean Park Pier offered: roller coasters and midway games. Cards from Vera-May Lewis collection. Published by Western Publications and Novelties

Ocean Park Pier – a Feast of Thrills

Ocean Park Pier was like a fantasy kingdom to me as a child. My sister and I had young parents. They had just turned 19 when I was born, and by 1945, at the end of the war, my youthful parents enjoyed the opulence of the pier. In fact, as the war ended there was a surge in attendance. My Ocean Park Pier was a feast of thrills.

It's true, the heydays of the waterfront amusement piers up and down the west coast were nearing their demise. Television, automobiles, and Disneyland would strike death blows in the next decades, but in the 40's and early 50's, I was the lucky recipient of all that they had been. I can close my eyes, inhale, and the memories return.

I can almost smell the cotton candy and hear the delighted squeals of the other children as we

crowded onto the boardwalk. Before we entered the noisy Midway, which led out to the pier, there had to be a first stop; the Arctic Ice Cream Emporium. It was a dreamy walk-up stand on the east side of the boardwalk across from the hilarious Laffing Sal. The booth was set up to appear as a scene in the frozen tundra. There were "penguins" about, and row upon row of "snow" and "icicles". My father would buy a cone for me, an early version of a soft-serve frosty. It always came with a cherry on top. With my cone in hand, we would cross the packed boardwalk and aim for the entrance.

There was no admission fee. On the left side of the entrance, stood Laffing Sal. She was a cackling, feminine robot. The stout animated figure sported a gap-tooth smile. She giggled and gyrated, welcoming patrons. In adulthood, I learned that there had been 300 such Laffing Sals across America between the 1930's through the 1950's, delighting children in amusement

Laffing Sal - 1940's

parks. This was long before Disney's animated characters were born. The sound of Sal's raucous cackling was all it took to turn on my own giggle machine. I could not walk past her without breaking up in my own delighted squeals. Just thinking about her still makes me smile. She never stopped!! Between the arctic ice cream and the giggling, the mood would be set for a high time.

By 1949, our mother had become the lead soprano for the Santa Monica Civic Opera Association, a role she would hold for the next 15 years. She was mostly in rehearsal on weekend nights, leaving our father in charge of us. He may have loved the rides more than we did. We were at the pier almost every weekend. A favorite ride was the Big Dipper rollercoaster. We would ride again and again. When we got older, we were brave enough to raise our arms up as we flew down the steepest tracks. Today, we credit our sensitive necks to the beatings they took on the rollercoaster!

The Fun House was a place where my sister and I could spend hours. I particularly delighted in trying to walk up the rotating wall of the big wooden barrel. I got pretty good at it too. I could go up about four feet before gravity would pull me back. Sometimes we would lose our step and just roll around the bottom of the barrel, laughing. There was a maze house with an uneven floor that was crazy to walk across. The mirrored corridor was intriguing because we could see hilarious distortions of ourselves: tall and skinny, wide and loopy, big headed, or skinny headed. All of it was to our great delight.

After a satisfying session in the Fun House we might make our way to the smaller Ferris wheel. That ride could be alarming because each car was under its occupant's control. One could throw a lever and the whole cage would roll upside down while the Ferris Wheel was climbing ever higher. It could be really daunting to hang upside down. When we had enough spinning to feel a bit seasick, we might go to one of the stands where we could throw darts at balloons to win gold fish, or race little electric horses around a track, sometimes we would get three balls for a dime and try to knock down a stuffed monkey. It was an exhilarating way to spend one's childhood weekends.

Mad Skills with Bumper Cars

With so much time spent at the amusements you can believe we got pretty good at them. I had not thought much about my bumper car prowess until it was put to the test. I have not spent time regaling my eleven grandchildren with my amusement park heroics. The day came when long hidden skills were showcased.

It was on my 17 year-old grandson's college trip that my amusement park prowess was revealed. It was the summer of 2012. My daughter, Julina, invited me to join them on their college visits. There were four of us; Jake, his 11 year-old brother, James, myself and my daughter Julina. I was delighted.

A few days into the road trip, after looking over UC Santa Cruz, we decided to visit the attractions at the Santa Cruz Boardwalk. The entire trip had been a wonderful chance to have my daughter and her two big boys to myself. On this day we easily found a parking place and ventured up the steps to the wooden boardwalk which lined the beach. A sign explained that this amusement area was the only one on the whole of the west coast that had been in continuous operation since it

Jake and his grandmother (Mimi) 2012

opened in 1907.

I felt like I had stepped into my past as I glanced around and saw two gigantic roller coasters, a big colorful arcade, the aerial tram over head, and the whirly ride. But mostly I saw the bumper car pavilion.

James was all about the merry-go-round, and since I truly was along for the ride, I agreed to a ride. After obtaining our tickets, we all climbed aboard our brightly colored horses. The bell clanged and we were off. I felt a bit like I was riding into my past, in a good way. I tried grabbing the brass ring and missed. A few more times around, and I caught the ring. However, I was too excited to throw it into the clown's open mouth. It was hilarious. Each time I missed, I was caught up laughing. My daughter was jubilant as she managed to hit the target. After many rounds and lots of laughter, the bell clanged again and the horses slowed to a stop. It had been fun.

As we walked away from the carousal, James exclaimed, "Mom, I'm ready for ice cream dots!"

I wasn't too sure what they were, when Jake challenged, "Not until I get you guys on the bumper cars!"

"I'm up for it!" I chimed in. I kept my thoughts to myself. My awkward showing with the merry-go-round rings had, perhaps, set my grandson up for a rude awakening regarding his grandmother.

We made our way to the bumper car pavilion. My strapping big boy, Jake, had no idea what was in store for him. How could he? I never talked about it. We quickly claimed our cars. The starting buzzer sounded and the electric floor became "hot." I could see Jake in front of me a few cars up. I slipped around a green one, gained speed and WHAM! I crashed into the back of his car. Shocked, he turned around to see that it was me, his gleeful grandmother, laughing like a maniac, I raced away to the safety at the perimeter of the floor.

I turned my head and caught a quick glimpse. Jake was in hot pursuit of me. The game was on! I swerved between a few little kids in slower cars and kept to the edge. Jake's face was all determination as he floored his pedal. He was coming for me, but suddenly the congestion in front of him forced him to slow down. I made a quick get-away. I kept my wits about me and slipped between the colorful cars until I was again behind him. Thud! I got him.

I imagine he was thinking, *"What? Not again!"* Our family is nothing if not competitive. With an even more resolute set to his shoulder, he took off in full pursuit of me, but by now I was way in front of him. Around and around the floor we chased each other. I could tell that he was serious about getting a shot at me, but I was too slippery. He seemed determined not to let his grandmother get the best of him.

I continued to keep to the edges of the floor, and then like a stealthy ninja warrior, I emerged from the cover of the other cars, to strike him yet again. He tried his hardest to reciprocate, but I was too fast and too sneaky. The ending clang sounded. Ha! My childhood strategy of cruising the periphery, until my target was within range had paid off.

As we reunited at the end of the ride, Jake slipped his arm around my waist. Julie linked her arm through mine. Jake summed up the afternoon, "Well, Mims, I had no idea that you had a secret life as a commando. That was some fancy car bumping!" He paused. "Lady, there's NO way this is over. There's going to be a rematch and watch out. I'm going to be coming for you!" teased Jake, his bright green eyes dancing with merriment.

James broke in, "So who's up for dipping dots?"

That day had reminded me how much our father had loved the bumping cars. He had been a devotee to all such amusements. By our teens, my sister, Jackie, and I had, with our father leading the charge, visited all the major amusement parks across the United States. I realize now, it was a rare kind of education, though my mad bumper car skills had not been much in demand until that day with Jake.

Gambling Ships in Santa Monica Bay

Across our childhoods, while we enjoyed the child-friendly land activities, thousands of adults sought entertainment on the off-shore gambling ships. Two such ships in the Santa Monica Bay began attracting patrons in the 1930's through the 1940's. A newspaper ad for one such ship, the S.S. Rex anchored off the coast of Santa Monica, stated:

> **There is only one Rex. Join the fun! THE WORLD'S LARGEST, MOST LUXURIOUS CASINO. PLAY to your heart's content in an atmosphere of unbridled luxury! Dine and Dance to the Rhythm of the Rex Mariners. Open 24 hours a day off Santa Monica. $.25 cents - round trip from Santa Monica Pier.**

Newspapers of the era describe the ships' owner, Anthony Cornero, as "The Admiral." Sometimes he was referred to as "Tony the Hat." He was an organized crime boss in Southern California from the 1920's through the 1950's. Anthony purchased the two ships, the SS Rex and the SS Tango, and began his floating gambling business. The ships catered to well-heeled crowds of 1000-3000 daily. They were open around the clock.

To ensure that the gambling, drinking, lavish shows, and restaurants continued undisturbed by law

The Rex Ship - Courtesy KCET

enforcement, Anthony anchored the floating casinos outside of the state's "three mile limit," where the law could not reach him. Shore boats off the Santa Monica Pier ferried patrons to and fro.

Before long, authorities in Santa Monica, became frustrated as anti-gambling groups brought pressure on them to stop the gambling. Many scrimmages ensued. There were attempted police raids met by firehoses from the ships. Finally, authorities decided to barricade access to the Rex. After eight days, Cornero surrendered. He was quoted as saying that he needed a haircut!

Ultimately the case regarding stopping the gambling was heard by the California Supreme Court and Tony Cornera lost his floating gambling business. He served no jail time and turned his energy to the more friendly environment of Las Vegas where he opened the Stardust Hotel. (*Time Magazine,* Aug. 19, 1946*)*.

An Enchanting Time in Southern California

Jackie and I were too young to know about gambling ships. In my search for Angelenos who remembered this time, I talked to my friend, Sallie Jac Shafer. During our telephone interview she explained that during her teens, she knew about those ships, that they had a *reputation.* She recalls that big stars came out to the area. Stars like Cab Calloway and His Orchestra who performed lavish shows, but then due to segregation, had problems finding hotel accommodations. She was not sure whether Cab played the ships.

DAILY CROWDS ON THE BEACH, OCEAN PARK

By the time Sallie was in her late teens, she discovered alluring entertainment a bit further inland. As the "boys" returned from WWII, she remembers wonderful dances at the Palladium in Hollywood and nights out in the big restaurants of the time: Chasen's, The Brown Derby, and Earl Carroll's night club. Chasen's, in particular, was famous as a celebrity haunt. Sallie had a wonderful friend, Eleanor Whiting, who was married to the famous song writer, Dick Whiting. Not only did Eleanor share celebrity stories, she knew through her husband's musical career, but Eleanor's sister, Margaret Young, was also a recording star. The famous singer, Johnny Mercer, in fact, was Margaret's Godfather. Johnny Mercer was a song writer, singer, and co-founder of Capitol Records. Clearly, Eleanor and Sallie enjoyed lots of insider celebrity stories. Sallie concluded by saying, "It was an interesting era in Los Angeles, and very fun!"

1926 Winter visit Venice Beach. Vera May right front with her son Raymond Junior

Carousel House Santa Monica Pier

Chapter Four

The People on the Benches of Ocean Park

"Action is the only remedy to indifference: the most insidious danger of all." Elie Wiesel, Nobel Peace Prize

My sister and I felt a sense of power when our parents deemed us old enough to ride the tram by ourselves to the Santa Monica Pier. I was eight and a half and Jackie was seven. We felt very grown up pocketing our dimes for the tram ride. We walked from 4411 Ocean Front Walk, on a Saturday or a Sunday to Windward Avenue where we caught the tram. Our destination was the checkerboard tables at the foot of the Santa Monica Pier in front of the merry-go-round house. We checked-in with our champion checker-playing grandfather, Big Ray. He would look up from his game and smile his toothless grin, introduce us to his fellow checker players, reach into the pocket of his dark suit and retrieve coins for us. We would exchange a hug and then scamper off to ride the merry-go-round for the next several hours. The checker players returned to trying to beat "Doc" at his game. He was said to be the best player in all of Los Angeles.

At the carousel, we quickly strapped ourselves onto our favorite horses. The bell would clang, and the distinctive organ sounds of the calliope music would fill the air. We arranged ourselves on the outside horses, practicing our balance, leaning out as far as possible, as the carousel would slowly begin to move. As it picked up speed, our excitement grew. Around and around we whirled, reaching our little-girl arms out to the tin ring-holder, hoping to be the recipient of the coveted brass ring!

We rode the merry-go-round so often on those golden days that catching the lauded brass ring, and getting a free ride, were frequent, exhilarating events.

People of the Benches

On those trips to find Big Ray and ride the merry-go-round, I was becoming more aware of my surroundings. As the tram passed Dudley Street a block or so up from Windward Avenue, I began to study the great numbers of old people dressed mostly in black, sitting peacefully, chatting with one

another along the boardwalk benches. My eight-year-old brain thought of them as "bench people." Though today, I appreciate and understand who they were, seventy years later, the idea of "bench people" is still in my mind. The women covered their heads with dark scarves. It was quite a strange contrast, old people in black, sitting, against a sea of active beachgoers in colorful clothing. When the tram slowed, I'd hear snatches of conversation. It was not English.

The Jewish Community of Venice

They intrigued me. Why were there so many of them? Why were they not acting the like other beach people? They seemed to sit all day. They were there when we rode to the pier in the late morning, and they were still there hours later when we returned. I didn't know much back then, but I knew enough to guess that they were refugees.

It was week ten of our mandatory government lockdown. The pandemic roared on. I had the luxury of time to research for some answers. My studies explained that the "bench people," were a part of a Jewish community which had settled along the ocean front back in the 1920's. They were mostly working-class people who provided the commercial and service infrastructure which supported the amusement industry. They called themselves "Venice Jews" and they were part of a dynamic Orthodox congregation, Mishkon Tephilo, founded in 1918.

The Venice Jewish community emerged with a distinct ocean centric orientation. In the early 1920's, two-thirds of Jewish households in Venice and Ocean Park were located within three blocks of the beach. All were within three-quarters of a mile of the beach.

Between 1880 and 1914, over two million Jews from Eastern Europe, particularly Russia, immigrated to the US. As the century turned, Jews from this mass migration began to find their way into Southern California. Those immigrants were likely to be acculturated to American ways. Surely their grown children, second generation in the United States, and fully Americanized, would have been attracted to the many economic opportunities offered in temperate Southern California. In 1920 there were 20,000 Jewish people in Los Angeles and by 1930 their population had grown to 70,000.

The Jewish "Main Street"

The boardwalk along the beach, known officially as Ocean Front Walk, was "Main Street" to Jewish Venetians. [As the literature refers to them.] Academics explained that "Main Street" is a concept of great cultural importance. It is a "setting in which social drama unfolds." (Shevitz. P.130). In less academic terms, the boardwalk is where the Jewish community *lived*. It was the stuff of life for them.

As a little girl, I was aware of the synagogue on the boardwalk, but that was all. I see now that it has always been the center of the Jewish community life. It was then, and is now, a senior center as well. That explains why there were so many old people.

Venice Jewish "Main Street" from A. Shevitz report - L.A. County Museum of History. c 1922.

On our recent walking tour of Venice, Ken and I went to the door of the synagogue. A sign read: "Shul closed for renovations." I had to look up the difference between "Shul" and "Synagogue."

"Shul" is a Yiddish word referring to a house of worship among orthodox sects. "Synagogue" is the term used for a house of worship which cuts across *all* Jewish sects. I noted the Shul in Venice has a clever slogan. "It is cool at the Shul." I Googled the saying and the Venice Shul immediately came up. I visited its homepage: *"Welcome to the Shul on the Beach! We invite you to visit our historic Synagogue on the Venice Boardwalk. We welcome Jews of every background to join our 'user friendly' traditional Orthodox services and celebrations."*

Our friend Manya of the Opera Company

A few weeks ago, I came across a captivating opera publicity photo of my mother and her best friend, Manya Hartmayer Breuer. The young women are posed in their opera costumes. I have vivid memories of visiting Manya's house on the boardwalk next to the beach front synagogue. I knew she was a Holocaust survivor, and I wondered why she chose to move to Venice? My research helped me to understand.

I called my 96-year-old mother to help me remember more about her friendship with Manya. She explained that she and Manya joined the Santa Monica Civic Opera Company at the same time in 1948. The opera company's director was glad to have two more singers to fill out the chorus. My mother and Manya actually first met on the stage in the back row of the chorus. Dressed in elaborate, long-skirted costumes, they were clueless about the storyline. There was a packed audience in Barnum Hall on the campus of Santa Monica High School. My Mom laughed a bit at the memory, "The two of us looked questioningly at one another. The plot was in Italian. We didn't know if we were supposed to be happy or sad chorus people? We couldn't help each other. We looked at the other singers, shrugged our shoulders, and did our best to fake it." That bewildering stage experience was the beginning of their life long friendship.

Both my mother and Manya were sopranos with much in common; beautiful young mothers in their twenties with little children. Across my childhood, our mother took us on frequent visits to Manya's home, where Jackie and I would play with her daughter Diana. I recall walking on the boardwalk past Windward and stopping at a brick apartment building next to the synagogue. We walked four steps up to Manya's family's apartment which was on the right side of the building. It had a picture window that looked out onto the sand. During that recent trip to Venice, Ken and I went to that apartment. It was a comforting feeling to see that it was just the same as in my memory.

Manya's Story

My mother reminded me that Manya devoted her life to ensuring that the cultural memory of the Holocaust would not fade. She was an adamant proponent of the *Never Again Movement,* and was a valuable resource for scholars. A Google search of Manya's work took me to a 1994 video-taped interview which she gave on the 50th anniversary of her liberation. It was bittersweet to see her beautiful face and hear her accented English as she shared her terrible story.

She was born in Berlin, Germany, in 1921 into a large family with brothers and a sister. She lost them all during the Nazi reign of terror. As a young adult, she and her father, along with others, escaped the concentration camps and attempted to flee on foot over the Alps into Italy. The Nazi soldiers were right behind them. It was cold and hard climbing through the mountains. Manya recalled that her father could see that they would be captured. He gave her his shirt to keep her warm and sent her forward to freedom. He surrendered himself to the soldiers to protect her.

Once she got to Italy, she found her way to a convent where she hid. She was hungry, scared, and alone, knowing that at any moment the Nazis could storm the door and kill her. She suffered a broken heart for the loss of her family. She knew they were gone; her sister had been alive when she was forced into a box which had been nailed shut. She was left to die.

While Manya remained hidden and hungry in the convent in Rome, a Jewish American journalist,

Ruth Gruber, worked through American political channels to try to rescue Holocaust survivors. Ruth faced huge political hurdles. America was seriously ethnocentric, and unfriendly to the idea of accepting refugees. Politicians did not want to risk their votes. Finally, in the midst of the war, in 1943, Ruth was granted permission to go to Europe. It was a top secret mission and she was limited to bringing just 1000 refugees back to the United States on a medical ship. Manya was among them.

When they arrived in New York, they were taken by train to a camp at Oswega, in upstate New York on the shores of Lake Ontario. There they stayed for the duration of the war, unable to leave the heavily guarded camp.

Ruth Gruber's story of bringing the survivors home is an award-winning book: *Haven: The Dramatic Story of 1,000 World War II refugees and How They Came to America.* (2010). It is also a 2001 film aired on CBS and an Emmy Award winner. It is available to watch on Amazon Prime. Manya's character has an important role in the film.

In her 50-year anniversary interview, Manya explained that coming to America was a dream. She married a fellow survivor during their stay in Oswega, and in fact, she gave birth to her daughter, Diana, at the camp. Manya was particularly proud to be the mother of two Americans. She concluded her interview by saying that "we are all the same. We are born and we die. There is no place for hate."

Dorothy Lewis left, Manya Breuer 1950's   Santa Monica Civic Opera Company

Manya raised her family, sang opera, curated in an art gallery, and worked to make the world a safer place. I think she lived a remarkable and fulfilling life. She and my mother stayed in touch across the years until 2018 when Manya passed away. I feel humbled to have known her. She leaves a rich legacy of courage. She proves the power of a single voice. I know that in her heart she was speaking out for her parents, her brothers, her sister and the millions of others who perished at the hands of the Nazi terrorists.

The people of the benches found safety and community in one another. Surely, Manya and her family found their way to the beachfront in Venice, California, because it was welcoming. It was a place where she could find solace, a place like home. Perhaps she found something of the family she had lost all those years before.

Manya's Venice Boardwalk apartment - front right 1950's. photo 2020

Fleeing the Bolsheviks

While on a walk with my golden retrievers, my thoughts kept going back to the old people sitting on the benches. With the clarity of time, I realized that in the 1940's, only some twenty-five or so years had passed for the early refugees that had escaped pre-Nazi Europe. The Bolshevik Revolution of 1917 was a dangerous place for Jews. I thought about my friends, Marc and Renee Perlman and what they had once shared with me. We had been trip mates on a tour of Moscow and St. Petersburg about eighteen years ago. On the trip, an incident occurred which I have never forgotten.

One night we had attended a folk performance and had chosen to walk the dark streets of St. Petersburg back to our hotel a mile away. As we walked along, a drunken man interrupted our journey. He jostled us. Marc intervened and corrected him in Russian! *Russian?* All three of us were surprised to hear our very American Marc, speaking Russian! He was as taken aback as we were. He confessed that he had not known those words were still in his head. He explained that as a child his mother had spoken to him in Russian, but that was a long time ago. He shared his parents' story with me as we continued our walk.

Russian Orthodox Church - St. Petersburg

It was after the Russian Revolution of 1917. The Tsar had fallen. Jews were not allowed to attend school. His future parents were students. Nightmares of bloody pogroms must have been fresh in their memories. During the years of 1903-1906 there were horrific massacres across Russia. There had been many across history, but in this one, some 2000 Jews were slaughtered.

Marc explained that his parents made their way to safety in Prague. They were determined to complete their educations. His mother, Sima Pasteur, graduated from medical school in 1927. She married her fellow student, Leo Perlman. Marc was born in Prague in 1934 where the family made a well-to-do life. Marc's father, Leo, was intuitive. He could feel the stirrings of trouble as Hitler's extreme ideas began to gather momentum. He strategically began making business trips to America. He was establishing himself with an insurance business in case he had to get his family out of Prague. When Marc was four years-old, his parents realized that they had to leave. Marc has a memory of Hitler's soldiers as they goose-stepped across the cobblestone streets of the city. He recalls a whooshing sound as the Nazi bullet canisters hit against their backsides. What a remarkable memory from a four-year-old.

I chatted with Renee on the phone to make sure I recalled the story correctly. She explained that Marc was in a Zoom session with one of his patients. Renee reminded me that Marc's parents "got the last boat out of Prague." It seems the Nazis were on their heels.

I thought of the productive life he, Dr. Marcel Perlman, Professor Emeritus, Yeshiva University, has lived. He is a psychologist and was a professor in New York City. I thought of his sixty-year-long career, dedicating his life to students, of his unfailing contribution to humanity. I thought of Renee, a life-time educator, a devoted mother and grandmother. I smiled at her humorous ways. How could it be that millions of such people have been murdered? It is not possible to estimate the loss of what their contributions could have meant to humanity.

Donna, Renee & Marc, Perlman, & Guide
2002 St. Petersburg, Russia

Tears filled my eyes. This line of thinking was not doing me any good. The dogs and I had made it to an open space. I bent down and undid their leashes so they could run free. I needed to stop thinking about freedom and tyrants.

A few days later, I felt that I had gained a better understanding of the people on the benches and what they had survived. I turned my attention to a different aspect of the culture of the Jews on the benches.

I had the opportunity to interview my friends John and Charlie Clifton who also grew up in Venice, during the same time in history as I did. However, unlike my sister and me, the Clifton boys interacted with the seniors on the benches. I invited them to my patio to hear their stories. We practiced social distancing to protect our health from the coronavirus. I turned on my tape recorder.

Latchless Kids

The Clifton brothers did not simply grow up in Venice, they were third generation Venetians. Their cultural memory goes back a long way. I will share more of their family stories later on in Chapter Seven. Ken joined us on the patio. The mood was light on a warm May morning. Ken and the Clifton brothers had all enjoyed surfing the waves that rolled through Ballona Creek before the breakwater was built. They had a lot to chat about.

John and Charlie laughed out loud as they recalled how, as kids, they ranged free, as had my sister and I. They joked, "We were LATCHLESS kids!" I laughed too, as people talk about "latchkey" kids who come home to an empty house. These boys were free to wander all day, every day of summer and weekends.

Their mother had one admonition. "Do not go under the Ocean Park Pier!" There had once been trouble there, maybe a murder. The boys minded her. Their attention was often focused on activities that could bring in a little cash.

One of their most profitable endeavors was to ride their bikes from home, a few blocks east of Lincoln Boulevard off Washington, all the way to the Santa Monica Pier. They would fish off the end of the pier, set up a little table with their haul, and the Jewish people would stroll out and buy the fish; five cents for a small one and ten cents for a bigger one. The boys would wrap the fish in newspaper, keeping their eyes out for the Fish and Game warden. John added, "If we caught a nice bonito or two big mackerel there was a place at the foot of the pier where they would trade two good fish for a smoked fish."

When the mackerel were running, Charlie would go out on the half-day boat and get his gunny sacks full. If he had two or three bags of mackerel, a deckhand would help him get them off the boat onto the dock. Three bags were too much to carry, so Charlie would tuck into a corner of the dock, behind a piling, away from the warden. Charlie added, "He was on to me, but he *never* caught me with a hand full of nickels and dimes. He was a mean guy."

"The Jewish people would find their way to me and buy out my fish. Sometimes, if I only had one bag, I'd drag it slowly along the boardwalk in front of all the folks on the benches. The old people were happy to see me. By the time I got to Windward Avenue, my bag would be empty."

John and Charlie remembered that the men wore transparent green visors and often were sitting in their covered three-wheeled electric carts. When they reached into their pockets for the coins, sometimes the boys would glimpse the long row of tattooed numbers on the inside of their left wrist. Those numbers suggested some unspeakable things, something awful that kept the tattoos in the boys' memories across all these years.

Charlie and John also remembered biking along the boardwalk. They would be towing their "rickshaws" with their surfboards attached. If they might accidentally get too close to the people on the benches, an old lady might reach out with her cane and smack the back of the surfboard, a warning, "*You kids better keep your distance from our knees!*"

Taken up by his memories, John suddenly asked, "Do you remember all the Jewish grocery stores and small businesses along that section of Ocean Park? One of them had a pickle barrel out in front. We'd pick out a big dill pickle and buy a bagel. It was heaven. When we were older, sometimes there'd be an older boy who could buy a beer and we'd sip beer and eat those bagels and pickles! Wow.

Delicious!" John smiled at the memory.

We had a wonderful time that day sharing memories of Venice in the 1940's into the 1960's. We came away from the conversation with a realization that we had experienced something special; a time and place when little kids could roam free and it was possible to be "latchless" kids.

Clifton boys on their dad's fishing boat

Donna and Jackie Easter Sunday, 1948

Chapter Five

Frenzy for Drilling Oil

Venice became the fourth most productive oil field in California.

One summer day in about 1945, our father climbed up high onto the oil derrick next door, something he did with regularity. This provided a vantage point from which he could see miles of shoreline; Catalina off in the distance, and the mountains of Santa Monica. A few times he spotted a sea lion stuck on the shore that needed rescue. One time he saw that a wrecked power boat had washed up in front of our house. On this day, his perch allowed a gruesome discovery. He spotted a human body which had floated onto the beach. The police were called. There was a big commotion. Jackie and I were scared. We girls were ordered to wait inside until the authorities finished up. We never did learn much more about it; we didn't *see* anything, but the magnitude of it … a *dead body!!* The mystery of it all stayed with us for a long time.

The oil well next door not only offered our dad a vantage point to scout out the beach, it also provided a consistent source of activity as trucks and workers checked on the status of the equipment twice a day. The wells were a constant in our lives.

Oil is Discovered in Venice

In December of 1929 oil was discovered on the Venice Peninsula and a wild oil drilling frenzy followed. Our family arrived in the area in the summer of 1945. By this time, the wells had found their stride and were working hard. They whooshed and pumped up and down every minute of every day of my childhood. It was routine. I did not like, nor hate it. It just was.

The other night Ken and I were watching *The Rookie* on television. The bad guy lured our hero, the Rookie, into the oil fields of the Baldwin Hills of Los Angeles. "Ken, look! Oil wells!" I'd exclaimed. I had already begun to share this story with you, and I had been focused on oil drilling. The sudden appearance of those wells on the TV screen was startling, like seeing an old friend you hadn't seen in a long time, an old friend you hadn't even *thought* about in a very long time.

Ken noticed my interest and offered, "How about if I take you there on our Thursday adventure?"

"Great idea!" I had quickly agreed. We had been leaving the house on Thursdays when the house cleaner was in for safety reasons.

So last week I met up with my old friends, oil wells. It was an odd reunion as they just pumped along, oblivious to my enthusiasm. However, it did remind me of their ubiquitous presence in my growing years.

When our family moved to Venice there were, perhaps, 450 wells pumping out "liquid gold." None of us thought much about it. I believe my grandparents were able to purchase the vacant lot for a cheap price because of the well next door. They paid $1000 during war time. It's interesting to think about. They purchased a vacant lot on the ocean front with a mansion on one side, and an oil well on the other. It was a microcosm of what had taken place.

Donna & Jackie moved to beach 1945 – War surplus yellow raft on which their parents rode waves.

From Fantasy to Science Fiction

So far we have learned of Kinney's fantasy turned into reality; the stuff of legends. Kinney took a swampland and created something almost other-worldly, where tens of thousands of people spent their

Venice Oil Field c. 1930's

leisure time in gondolas and enjoying state-of-the art attractions. There aren't too many such stories, especially over a hundred years ago.

By 1929 the Venice Peninsula, which is the ocean front south of Washington Boulevard, had become a quiet residential area where stately homes dotted the ocean front as well as the side streets which were known as "courts." Garages were accessed through alleys behind the homes, thus providing the homes with the luxury of facing the tidy little pedestrian walkways.

The international stock market collapsed at the end of 1929. Wall Street executives were said to jump out of windows. Economic devastation fell across the land. Oddly, simultaneously, in December of 1929, oil was discovered in Venice. The discovery set off an explosion of oil drilling. Big oil companies immediately sent representatives door-to-door to buy up drilling rights from the property owners. Homeowners beseeched the City Council to overturn zoning ordinances and allow drilling beneath their properties.

Within months a large swath of the pristine beach line, south from Washington all the way into Playa del Rey, became a noxious industrial oil field. A field so prolific that within a few months a single oil well churned out 5000 barrels a day! Reports claim that by June of 1930 the wells across the field were producing $75,000 per week in oil. The Venice fields became the fourth most productive in all of

California. Soon the area became so toxic that the elementary school, Nightingale, where I later attended, had to be closed for the safety of the children.

I'm particularly interested in the fact that the property owners of the coveted beach properties were so quick to throw over their pristine, resort-like living, for the profits of what lay below their dirt. The derricks came up so fast that the newspapers referred to the petroleum zone as the "destruction of Venice."

In 1926 Venice was annexed into Los Angeles. At the time California had few limits on a property owner's rights to exploit mineral resources. However, though Los Angeles had zoning regulations which prohibited drilling in residential and commercial areas, public opinion was strongly in support of getting the oil. Oil companies bought up drilling rights, and homeowners begged for drilling permits, worrying that the oil would dry up before they realized their fortunes. The Law of Capture allowed homeowners and oil prospectors to move forward.

Venice City Council members were on board for drilling [though they must have merely been an advisory body to the official City Council of Los Angeles]. My land-use attorney son, Rick, explained to me that in the early years of the 20th Century, zoning ordinances did not have the strength they have today.

J.C. Barthel, a Venice council member stated "[oil drilling is] one of the most popular issues with the greatest unanimity of opinion I've ever seen." A group of 5000 Venice and Playa del Rey residents petitioned the council to "eliminate restrictions on oil drilling in Venice." In another demonstration of

unity, "a big group of 3000 Venice residents went even further and demanded an end to restrictions on oil drilling everywhere in the City of Los Angeles."

They argued that landowners had specific rights, based upon the Law of Capture, to exploit the minerals beneath their properties and to lease their property to whomever they wished. There were stories of council members' wives petitioning for drilling permits in their maiden names. The rush was on to drill.

Opponents did their best to make the case that wells were public nuisances; that they infringed on the property rights of others. A major argument was the fact that one of the great drivers for bringing annexation to Venice was to benefit from the more strict zoning ordinances of Los Angeles. They urged Los Angeles council members to fully enforce the zoning to protect the public. Their voices were drowned out by the noise of the property owners who saw dollar signs in their dreams. (Elkind, p. 83. *Journal of American History, June 2012)*

The Los Angeles Times, June 29, 1930 ran this story:

Today oil derricks stand like trees in a forest...Steam pile drivers roar on many a vacant

lot…one hundred and eighty permits to drill for oil have been given and twenty-five more are in procedure. If this fever continues, as it gives every indication of doing, one reasonably may expect to see virtually the entire water front line of private properties from Washington Street to Sixty-sixth avenue …dotted with a line of oil derricks. (Elkind. P 82).

Those drilling opponents raised the problems inherent in "town lot field" drilling. "Town lots" are oil fields with derricks which are erected on small house lots. In other words, it meant drilling for oil in residential neighborhoods. The wells suffered frequent oil spills, fires, gushers, explosions, and blowouts. The high gas pressure beneath the earth was needed to extract the oil. That gas was part of the problem. There were additional issues such as delays in pipeline construction and the arrival of tankers for carrying the oil away.

I read of a case where a Venice oil producer purposely allowed a well to spew oil wildly, far and wide, as part of a publicity stunt. He wanted to prove the unlimited availability and the high profitability of drilling for oil. Perhaps, too, he wanted to make existing residents think twice about continuing to live on oil rich land. In these town lot fields, those dangers were exacerbated by nearby homes. Our home was perhaps twenty feet from the oil well. It was dangerous but we didn't give it a thought.

As the backlash continued across the next decade, some of the big oil companies began to use conservation methods such as watch dogging the natural gas which made the extraction possible. Other measures proposed were creating a minimum distance between wells and homes, camouflaging the derricks, and profit sharing among the lease holders.

Some of those measures would have decreased the negative impacts of the wells in Venice, but folks were not going for it. Big Oil was on board with conservation but there were too many smaller, independent companies that were not on board.

As the decade of the 30's moved forward, lawmakers in Los Angeles in cooperation with the Playground and Recreation Commission, began to realize the horror of what had happened. Venice had become horrendously polluted.

The City Council Proposes Oil Wells on the Beach

The Venice Council proposed: **that the City of Los Angeles lease the beach itself for drilling and use the money to buy more pristine shorelines elsewhere. The decision makers were annoyed that not only were the oil companies ruining the beaches, but they were encroaching on oil that belonged to the public. Their hope was that by leasing the actual beach in Venice, some benefit would come to the public.**

Thankfully citizen groups were opposed to leasing the beach. In addition, a powerful movie star, Lewis Stone, who owned a beach house, brought a lawsuit against the City. Stone argued that derricks on the sand constituted a "public nuisance." The court ruled in his favor, though of course, derricks continued to line the ocean side of Speedway, at the edge of the sand.

The debate continued. Standard Oil successfully backed a proposition, Proposition 4, which would allow "slant drilling," a process that could access oil under the ocean. Cleverly, the proposition earmarked a portion of the profits for state parks. It passed without a hitch, thus allowing "slant drilling" to be legal. Slant drilling would continue for the next several decades.

The only victory for the environmentalists was the prohibition of oil derricks on the beach. As the 1940's rolled in, public sentiment began to move away from the popularity of oil extraction. More citizens were calling for clean-ups, that is, until Pearl Harbor.

The bombing of Pearl Harbor opened the door for more support for oil drilling; the war effort needed oil. Shell Oil found a sliver of unincorporated land adjacent to homes in Los Angeles which had not been tapped. They requested a permit to drill. It was denied by Los Angeles Mayor Fletcher Bowron. Scores of additional drilling permit requests came up all around Los Angeles. Bowron and the other leaders held fast, as resident sentiment was on their side against more drilling in residential areas.

However, the federal government was too powerful to ignore. The Petroleum Administration for the War, the War Productions Board, and the U.S. Navy, all pressured local government officials, insisting that oil was needed to support the war effort. Thus, oil drilling rigs invading neighborhoods, and fields such as Venice, continued to drill. The citizenry supported the war and viewed the drilling as another necessary sacrifice.

The problem was that long after the war ended, drilling continued. Some concessions were made for the public good such as remediation for noise and fire. Other conservation measures were adopted, and

oil drilling continues.

Across the next decades, into the early 1960's, the Venice fields would be a source of conflict. The argument is a broader one over personal property rights versus the public esthetic. The fact that at this writing in 2020, there are still so many productive oil fields adjacent to residential neighborhoods in Southern California is proof that the public esthetic has not won out.

In any event, by the time I went off to USC in 1962, the Venice field had mostly dried up, and over the next ten years, the last of its wells would be capped. Venice and I sort of grew up together, moving on at the same time. Of course, my moving on meant that when my new husband and I purchased a home in 1965 in Huntington Beach, we had found ourselves living not all that far from yet another oil field! The cliffs along the coast of Huntington Beach were an important oil drilling field.

Oil Rich Los Angeles Basin

It is not lost on me that one of our frequent childhood adventures was to visit La Brea Tar Pits. They were only a mile away from our grandparents' Los Angeles home. Back then, there was no museum, just big pits secured by chain link fencing sprawled across a park near Wilshire Boulevard. Our grandparents were eager that we understood that great animals had roamed the Los Angeles basin for eons. Some became trapped in the tar and preserved. We learned that the pits provided a fossil record like no other place, that the tar pits are unique in the world and have been continually excavated since 1906. It was fun to learn that La Brea means "the tar" in Spanish.

It could not have been a surprise then when in 1892, gold prospector, Edward Doheny, discovered an abundance of oil in a Los Angeles City Oil Field. That find led to similar discoveries in the surrounding areas. Those fields became the top producers in California. By 1895 they accounted for half of the state's oil production. The Los Angeles City Oil field today covers a large territory in mid-city of Los Angeles, extending from just south of Dodger Stadium west to Vermont Avenue encompassing an area of four miles in length by a quarter mile in width. That field is mostly inactive today, with just one functioning well.

Oil seeping at the La Brea Tar Pits

Oil wells were a common fixture of my childhood. There were forests of them around the low hills of Los Angeles, in Long Beach at Signal Hill, in Baldwin Hills, and along the cliffs in Huntington Beach.

Our grandparents lived in the Fairfax

District of Los Angeles, across the street from the Farmer's Market. We loved to visit Farmer's Market which was next to Arthur Gilmore's Stadium and original gas station. Gilmore had been a dairy farmer who got lucky when he struck oil. By 1905 he rid himself of the dairy and opened Gilmore Oil Company with the slogan, ***"Someday you will own a horseless carriage. Our gasoline will run it." Gilmore Oil.***

He was true to his word. As the automobile took over, Gilmore expanded his business to having some 3000 gas stations across the West Coast. His was considered the West's premiere gasoline brand. As Los Angeles grew and homes began to crowd around Gilmore's wells, he converted one field into a stadium and built a miniature car racing track and a baseball field.

Gilmore Stadium became a place to go and was heavily advertised. My mother recalls her parents loading her into the car and "driving all the out to Fairfax. It was quite a trip from Western Avenue. My father loved to watch baseball there." Today there is an interesting display of Gilmore's pumps and memorabilia at the Farmer's Market.

California's economy is powered by oil and gas. California produces 463,000 barrels of oil a day making it the 6th largest producer in the United States. It consumes 1.8 million barrels a day, which forces the importation of three times more oil and gas than it produces. The oil production business has been an essential element in our economy. Of course, there has been controversy.

Across the settling of Los Angeles, the tar itself has caused trouble in other ways. My good friend Janet Harris Tonkovich recalls that her great grandfather, a sheep rancher in what is now northern Orange County, had so many problems with his sheep getting black tar all over their wool that he had to sell-off the Brea section of his ranch land. The gooey stuff was bad for the wool business!

These days Brea housing developers are eyeing the oil fields and dreaming of housing developments. *From drilling to dwellings: Housing plans for Brea's last big oil field move forward.* "After 100 years of oil production the droning swish and rhythmic bobbling of horse heads in eastern Brea could be replaced by the clatter of earth movers…as a housing development would be coming." (Robinson,

Baldwin Hills Oil Field - June 2020 - Los Angeles Oil Field

December 28, 2018, *Orange County Register*).

As California's population continues to grow from the 40 million it is today to the 60 million projected in the not too distant future, clearly the wells and drilling will give way to other, less invasive technologies. New uses will be found for the land.

California enjoys an economy equal to that of many countries. If we were a sovereign nation, our economy would be ranked 5th place in the world. That is a very big deal.

The oil and tar have been a part of California's story since the very beginning. Without it we would not have the fossil records we have, the Indigenous People would not have had it to waterproof their boats, and the vast benefits from our oil production would not have been realized. It has simply been a part of the Southern California story.

There was not a beach day in my growing up, that we did not have to get the turpentine out and clean all the tar off our feet. It was a fact of life.

Donna & Jackie c. 1946 in front of house

Donna in front yard 1946

Donna at age 11 – Not always a serious-minded girl.

77

1940's snow at the beach. Jackie above. Note oil field in back.

Mrs. Moore's home next door. Girls were playing outside of their front yard.

Chapter Six

Ballona Wetlands

The heart of the Ballona Wetlands is the coastal salt marsh, the crown jewel,
which requires oceanic tidal changes. Ballona Wetlands website.

It is week eleven of our isolation orders as I write this. The world is beginning to open up. Southern Californians are now allowed to park at the beaches, but they are for active use only! Sports and schools are still closed. None of this concerns me as my thoughts turn to Venice and its wetlands. It was just two weeks ago when Ken and I made a second research trip back to my youth. On that day we drove to Playa del Rey and parked our car next to the beach. I wanted to revisit the old Ballona Creek Bridge.

Old Ballona Creek Bridge

It was a beautiful day, early enough that not many bikers, nor joggers were out and about. Ken and I walked to the bridge. We stood against its old cement railing and looked east, down Ballona Creek. Ken smiled and I knew he was reliving one of his surfing exploits, the waves carrying him under the bridge and along the creek.

Today, the bridge is a something of a dead end; there's no longer vehicular, or pedestrian access across the marina entrance to Pacific Avenue on the Venice Peninsula. The bridge leads only to a paved bike path along the berm of the harbor entrance which takes one to the luxury marina homes.

It was quiet. I took it all in. Across my girlhood the bridge was the only southern access to Venice. This was long before the marina channel was dug. I pulled the peace in around me; took a deep breath of cool salty air. I could almost hear the echo of the voices of the ancient people who once inhabited this area.

Bike path along Marina Channel

The Indigenous People

The Indigenous People of the Los Angeles Basin were the Tongva. They, along with their Chumash neighbors, were the most powerful Indigenous People to inhabit Southern California. At the time of the arrival of the Europeans, the Indigenous population is thought to have numbered from 5,000 to 10,000 in Southern California.

I could visualize them along the creek making their way out into the ocean in their big rowing canoes. They were adept at salvaging logs which washed up on the shore, carving them into planks, and crafting large seafaring boats. The boats, *Ti'at,* were twenty feet long, ten feet wide, and could hold ten men. The boats allowed important trading between the Channel Islands, where their people also dwelled.

The Tongva culture was well developed. They had lived in the Los Angeles basin for over three thousand years, migrating from the interior desert, and displacing an earlier population of Hokan people. They are thought to have pushed the Hokan people out, or to have absorbed them. The Tongva spoke a Shoshonean dialect. Having become a maritime people, they prized the extensive wetlands area,

harvesting from both the land and sea.

A recent collaborative project was the creation of a "baby Ti'at" canoe for teaching purposes. Acjachemen, Chumash, and Tongva tribal members came together for the construction of this authentic canoe. Made of redwood, the one pictured here is from the KCET, 2019, documentary on traditional boat building. It is a much smaller vessel than the seagoing boats created by the Indigenous People.

Ken and I stood silently in the cool morning lost in our own thoughts. As I looked eastward, I imagined the Tongva village of about 100 inhabitants situated where Playa Vista is today. I could visualize the women dressed in garments of mashed bark or rabbit fur. The men might have worn a loin cloth or gone naked, as did the children. Perhaps a family would be coming out of their tule and reed hut. The cook fire would be going nearby. Possibly the day would be one where the steelhead trout were spawning up the creek. Maybe a bear or two would have lumbered down from the Santa Monica mountains to feast on the trout, making themselves fair game for the Tongva hunters.

Anthropologists believe that native people arrived in North America, about 13,000 years ago. They probably crossed the Bering Land Bridge from Asia, migrating south along the coast of the continent in their canoes. Describing her culture, Tongva educator, Cindi Alvitre, explained, *Water is sacred, water is life, water is us, water is everything."* (KCET program 2019).

When Spanish explorers, Gaspar de Portola´ and his men rode through the Los Angeles area in 1769, the diarist, Father Juan Crespi, described the natives as friendly. He further noted that they were "blond, short and sturdy," their skin appearing lighter than that of people in Mexico and South America. The women were known to rub red ocher on their skin to protect it from the sun. They also knew to use urine to rid themselves of hair lice. Perhaps the acid in the urine lightened the hair.

The Tongva occupied a big territory which extended from Mount Wilson, 40 miles to the east, north

Baby *Ti'at* seagoing boat — Rowed to Avalon.

to Malibu, and south to Laguna Beach. I enjoyed imagining the everyday life of the early people who lived here, where I had lived, adjacent to the wetlands.

More Recent Uses of the Wetlands

Ken reached for my hand and asked, "Do you want to walk for a little while?" We crossed the bridge and turned along the bike path toward the marina. "Ken, you see those homes there? That's where one of my favorite places once stood."

"I remember." His eyes twinkled knowingly. He knew of my crush on the very famous movie cowboy, Hopalong Cassidy. He squeezed my fingers as we strolled through the morning air. My thoughts slipped to that coveted memory. I had been eight-years-old. It was the day I met Hoppy in person!

Hopalong Cassidy was a cowboy character played by actor William Boyd in the movies and television. He was immensely popular, riding across American television and movie screens for forty years. William Boyd was the first actor to successfully transition from film to television. He was a sensation; a hero to boys and girls who wanted to be like Hoppy. Boys wore big tall black "Hoppy" hats and little girls carried lunch pails with his picture on them. We have a picture of Ken in such a hat.

When Hoppyland opened a few blocks from our house, in 1950, you can imagine how thrilling it was for us kids of the neighborhood. I felt excited just remembering that time. Back then, the area that

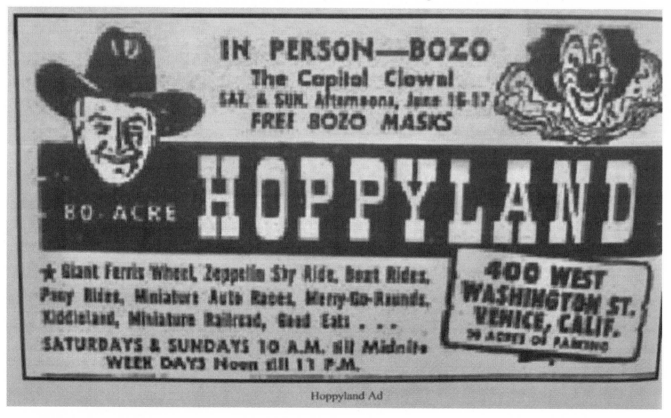

Hoppyland Ad

today is the beautiful Marina del Rey was nothing more than a swampy place with weeds and a local dumpsite. It was part of the La Ballona Wetlands. There was a dirt road off Washington Boulevard leading into it, just before the Grand Canal. Gardeners and construction workers would haul loads of trimmings, demolition materials, and trash, to the area where it was burned.

Oddly enough, no doubt due to low rents, an amusement park was created next to the dump. As an eight-year-old, I thought of it as a captivating kingdom. It was called 'Hoppyland.' It was something like a low-end fun zone with rides, cotton candy, and occasional appearances of Hoppy himself. It was a strange location to be sure, however, it was very near our house, and we kids did not care where it was. Hoppyland was a thrilling place to spend time.

Before that certain day with Hoppy, I had a serious crush on another even more famous cowboy, Roy Rogers, and his palomino horse, Trigger. I was wild for them, the horse, the singing. All of it! They were bigger than life to me, but oh how fickle can be a child's heart. All that changed the day I met Hoppy. Our family was meandering past the merry-go-round, when suddenly Hoppy appeared right in front of me. I was stunned speechless. He stopped to meet us. There were greetings exchanged between the adults, and suddenly Hoppy bent down and kissed me on the cheek. I nearly swooned. After that, Hoppy was the object of my ardor for the next several years, and poor Roy Rogers slipped from first place in my heart. Meeting Hoppy was an incredible event, a moment of delight, which has stayed fresh in my memory across all this time.

Ballona Watershed

A half hour later, Ken and I returned to the car. We wanted to get a better look at the Ballona Wetlands which today cover almost 600 acres. That is a quarter of what it was in earlier times. California has lost more than 90% of its wetlands to urban development and pollution. The wetlands are important migratory stops for birds along the Pacific flight zone.

We drove past the sign: "State Ecological Reserve." I knew that as late as the 20th Century, La Ballona Wetlands included the creek which we had just left. It is where the Los Angeles River once drained. Interestingly, in addition to an extensive marsh area, there had once been a lake. I had seen photos of boaters and fisherman on "Lake Ballona." Locals called it "Mud Lake" and "Lake Los Angeles." My Venice friends tell me that what remains of it is a part of "Mother's Beach," located in the western corner of Marina del Rey.

Within minutes Ken and I were driving east on Jefferson Boulevard in the thick of the wetlands which extend to Lincoln Boulevard. I was looking for any sign of my father's old "shop." In 1949 he opened a used car and body shop on a quarter acre of land on Jefferson Boulevard between Lincoln Boulevard and

Playa del Rey. He rented the site from the Machado family of the old Spanish land grant. The shop was a garage constructed of cement blocks on a vacant lot on which he lined up cars he had for sale.

We pulled to the side of the road. I thought I was near what had been the site of the shop. We examined the acres of tall grass surrounding us. We hoped to discover any evidence that a business had once been established there. Nothing. The entire area is covered by heavy brush and has returned to its natural state.

The name La Ballona probably comes from the Spaniards. Perhaps, they spotted whales, *"ballena,"* frolicking at the mouth of the creek. Or they may have named it for "Bayona," Spain. Today locals pronounce La Ballona with the Anglicized "l" sound, while academics use the proper Spanish pronunciation, *"bay ona."*

My thoughts went back to the shop. It had been carved out of the Machado family's corn and celery fields. My sister Jackie and I spent endless hours scouting around those fields. Once we found a nest of baby mice in the brush. Their naked little pink bodies fascinated us. We were careful to protect them.

One of the most memorable activities we enjoyed was gathering up celery that had been left behind after the harvest. The Machado family invited us to pick whatever we wanted of the delicious vegetable. It was a treasure hunt, finding stalks we could take home. Often in the evenings, on the way home, we would stop at the Machados' produce stand, where they sold fresh corn.

As Ken and I sat in the car looking across at the natural wetlands, I could not help but recall another time I had come to check on this exact spot. That time was because there had been a serious flood. It was November of 1950. California was hard hit by excessive snow melt and rain. A statewide disaster was called. Unfortunately, the low-lying wetlands were soon underwater.

My father was worried about his tools, and the condition of his cars. He borrowed a canoe, and we paddled out onto a flooded Jefferson Boulevard, and to the shop. It was under about three feet of water and was a mess. Photos were taken that day to record the seriousness of the water damage. You can see me in the canoe. It was a day I have always remembered because how often in California does one paddle to work with their dad?

The pictures remind me how much I enjoyed the years going to the shop after school. Even though I was but a child, I appreciated the open spaces and natural habitat of the Ballona Wetlands. After a few years, our father was hired full-time in the aircraft industry, and the shop was closed.

Donna in canoe 1950 – Brownie camera photo

Flooded Shop 1950

Rancho La Ballona

I found that when Abbot Kinney purchased the swampy land for his Venice-of-America, it was part of the 14,000 acre Rancho La Ballona owned by Ygnacio and Augustin Machado and Felipe and Tomas Telemendes. When I learned that the Machados, whom we had known, were the descendants of the original land grant family, I felt a ripple of connection.

In 1820 Augustin Machado was permitted a land grant from the Mexican government. The land covered a vast area extending to what is today Culver City, all the way to Santa Monica. They became wealthy and had important political connections. There were marriages into the powerful Sepulveda and Avila families.

The rancho wetlands were a rich area with much variety; including freshwater ponds, alkali flats, and saltwater inlets. It was home to streams which coursed through the area fed by springs in the Hollywood Hills. The Los Angeles River was the largest supplier of its water. In 1825 flooding and earthquakes shifted its course away from Ballona Creek. The river jumped its banks and redirected itself toward San Pedro, twenty miles to the south. The wetlands were never quite the same after that because so much of its freshwater vanished.

Damage to the Wetlands

The Machado and Telemendes families used the land for grazing and farming. As the years passed, the hungry cattle began to destroy the natural environment. By the middle of the 19th Century, the gold rush attracted hordes of foreigners who often squatted on the wetlands, using them as they pleased. They hunted the beautiful birds for their feathers and sold them for plumage. The wetlands suffered more damage from their activities.

Across the later decades of the 19th Century, entrepreneurs tried numerous ventures in the area. One enterprising fellow created a port at the mouth of Ballona Creek which he named "Port Ballona." He built a wharf and rented out fishing boats. He managed to get the Santa Fe Railway to run a passenger train to the port. It brought adventure-seeking Angelenos from downtown. Ultimately, the port was destroyed by high tides and storms.

The port may have disappeared, but businessmen kept their attention on the area. As California turned to the 20th Century, hotels and businesses sprang up around the beach at the mouth of the creek. Vacationers came to enjoy the fresh air, and the frequently held boat races. It was during this time that the Ballona Creek bridge was constructed, connecting the southern area to the beach communities in the north.

The Pacific Electric Car eventually replaced the old Santa Fe Train. It ran across the wetlands parallel to Culver Boulevard. The tracks were laid on the berm which today is the heavily used trail, known to bikers and joggers as "Trestle Trail."

In the 1930's the upper Ballona Creek was channelized by the Civilian Conservation Corps, greatly increasing the inflow of ocean water further inland, while simultaneously reducing both the fresh and salt waters to the marsh. The channelizing of the waters, significantly damaged the marine habitat. To add insult to the marsh, oil was discovered on the Venice Peninsula, bringing pollution, and more damage.

Across the centuries, the wetlands have suffered changes in topography, land use, ownership and the need for urban development. All of which negatively impacted the natural environment.

Development on the Wetlands

In 1940, business magnate, pilot, movie mogul, and engineer, Howard Hughes bought up 340 acres of the marsh wetlands. Hughes would be awarded a federal contract to build airplanes large enough to transport troops to Europe. Thus he needed a factory and an airport, which he built on the site. The government cancelled the contract before Hughes completed his prototype aircraft. However, they were

Spruce Goose in Long Beach – news reel photo

willing to fund the completion of one plane, the "Spruce Goose." It was the first aircraft with a wingspan of 300 feet. Though it was considered a "boondoggle," requiring Hughes to defend himself in front of senate hearings, its exquisite wooden craftsmanship made it a popular tourist attraction. Known as a *flying boat*, it only flew once.

On November 2, 1947, in front of thousands of spectators, Hughes took the prototype into Long Beach Harbor for a test flight. The plane taxied on the water and suddenly lifted its wooden wings 70 feet above the water, and flew for a mile before landing. Its home was in Long Beach where it attracted attention, sitting in a massive white hanger situated near the long-time home of the famed ship, Queen Mary. In 1992 it was dismantled and moved to an air museum in McMinnville, Oregon.

The Hughes Aircraft Company went on to build many aircraft. It was a large multi-building complex, painted an odd light green color; it dominated the southern portion of the wetlands across my life until 1985. Upon Hughes' death in 1976, his heirs began plans to develop the area into a higher use. The planned community began in 2002. Today, a neighborhood with a population of 14,000, known as Playa Vista occupies the site. There are condominium buildings, office spaces, retail, restaurants, and parks.

Ecological Reserve

California purchased about 290 acres from the Hughes' heirs with the idea of protecting some of the wetlands. Playa del Rey, a neighborhood of the City of Los Angeles, donated more acres. Activists and environmental groups successfully advocated for the establishment of a designated State Ecological Reserve on what remains of the wetlands. California understands that wetlands provide stop-over wintering and breeding habitats for vast numbers of waterfowl.

The State of California owns the land. It is managed by the California Department of Fish and Wildlife. A conservancy has been established which supports the Reserve through private donations. The wetlands are being restored as an estuary for wildlife and marine species. Environmentalists report that once again, species of birds not seen in decades are returning; birds such as the Blue Heron and the Snowy Egret.

Ken started the engine. "Next time we visit here let's plan to walk some of these nature trails and enjoy the wildlife."

I smiled at him. "Ken, I was remembering that most of this area, all the way to Culver City was in agriculture when I was young. Strawberry and corn fields abounded. It must be a difficult balancing act between the need for urban development with the necessity for preserving open space for the future."

"Donna that was one of the most difficult challenges we had while I was on the city council in San Juan Capistrano; preserving open space and the hillsides when property owners were eager to sell to the highest bidder."

"So how exactly did our town manage to preserve so much?"

"Don't you remember? The residents voted in measures for agricultural preservation and open space. We passed ordinances against building on the ridgelines. We passed large bonds to buy private lands. It took all of us."

I thought that over for a while. It takes an army of concerned citizens to preserve the natural environment.

Ken headed the car toward Lincoln Boulevard. "So where to next?" He asked, smiling.

South side of Ballona Creek Channel. A stable was here in the 50's-60's. Playa del Rey. Our friends the Cliftons remember riding from here.

Chapter Seven

Portrait of a California Pioneering Family

'The family is one of nature's masterpieces." George Santayana

Forty-eight years ago, Ken and I longed to move our young family from the suburbs to a place with more open spaces. Perhaps, being raised, literally, on the edge of the continent, spoiled me for conventional living. I know I had been young at the beach, but for me *normal* was to enjoy wide stretches of ocean and sand as far as the eye could see, and to feel humbled by the infinite miles of glistening water before me. As newlyweds, we purchased a nice tract home in Huntington Beach and settled in. Soon three children arrived. After nine years it wore thin. Our dog lumbered through the block wall fence to confront the mail man. Ken was attempting to grow corn in our three-foot wide side yard. It was not working. We knew we needed room to sprawl out.

We moved to the greater outdoors of horse country, to San Juan Capistrano, California, located in south Orange County. Coincidentally, another young family moved into our rural enclave at the same time. They were the Clifton family; Sherry and John and their two boys. We immediately became friends, sharing our passions for the green hillsides, horses, and raising children. Within a short time, we learned that Sherry and John also grew up in Venice. We all had a lot in common.

As this writing project moved along, I asked John about his Ocean Park Pier memories. He quickly offered me a few

Donna and Ken Family moves to rural
San Juan Capistrano c. mid-1970's

91

funny stories from the past. I could see that he was a rich source of information about the Venice we had experienced growing up. I asked for an interview. John explained that his brother, Charlie, was the family historian and would be happy to join us. He added that their parents and grandparents had lived in and worked in Venice. The Clifton brothers held almost one hundred years of Venice history.

The Clifton Family: Southern California Pioneers

On a sunny May morning, John and Charlie Clifton arrived on our patio, wearing their masks against the coronavirus, and carrying an envelope stuffed with their family's historic documents. Ken joined us. We remained outside, following the CDC health guidelines, and situated our chairs a proper "social distance" apart. We soon removed our masks.

The first item they pulled out was a big 8 x 10 photo of their grandparents' 1940's Pier Café on the boardwalk near the Santa Monica Pier. As their family story unfolded, I observed that all of them, for generations, had worked. They worked and worked. I thought of my family and their pharmacies, my father's body shop, my mother at the playground, my maternal grandfather's house painting business and more. The families that settled California labored! It seems to me that the backbone of what has made California great, the fifth most powerful economy in the world, is a strong work ethic. People like Abbot Kinney, William Mulholland, D.W. Griffith, William Hearst, and other famous figures in the settling of Los Angeles garner much acclaim, but the working families deserve credit for their important contributions as well. I see the Clifton story as a story of California pioneers. In this case, Venice pioneers.

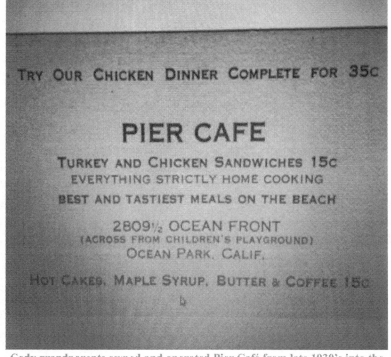

Cody grandparents owned and operated Pier Café from late 1930's into the 1940's

Fishing

John and Charlie Clifton began to share their tale. I turned on my recorder. The Cliftons' saga could be that of many Angelenos. In capturing their words on paper, I have tried to stay true to the style of their narrative. The account began with their grandfather, Daniel Clifton. Daniel was a railroad man, born in 1878, perhaps in Texas. He started his work life in California as a streetcar conductor on the 69th Street train in Los Angeles. He married Nellie Sexton from Indiana, and they had two boys, Ben and Chuck. Sadly, their grandfather, Daniel, was killed in 1921 in a horrible train accident. Nellie received $5000 in a death benefit from the Railroad and moved to 1811 Ocean Front Walk, Venice with her boys; 11 year-old Ben, and 8 year-old Chuck. It was up to the boys to support the family.

When John and Charlie's dad, Chuck, was just 12 years-old, he started what would become his lifetime career as a fisherman. By the age of 16, he kept a dory tied underneath the Venice Pier. He would take it out every day to earn enough money to support himself and his mom. Ben found work on an oiler that ran between Southern California and San Francisco and made his home in San Francisco. With the rapidly developing Depression, this left Chuck to bring in the living. To save on rent, in 1930, they moved to Linnie Canal where Nellie paid only $28 a month.

By this time the canals were in bad shape. The City of Venice had annexed with Los Angeles in 1926, hoping to solve the canal problem. They were filled with silt, oil pollution, and had a terrible stink when the Red Tide was in. Venice hoped that the greater resources of Los Angeles could manage a clean-out program.

Daniel Clifton - grandfather

The City of Los Angeles did provide a solution, a harsh one. By 1929, the City filled in, and paved over all seven of Kinney's original canals. The only remaining canals were, and are, the six built by another developer, adjacent to Kinney's canals. Those canals, in fact, remained a stinky problem for some forty more years. It wasn't until 1992 when the City of Los Angeles financed a large renovation project and rehabilitated the canal district that things began to improve. The grand plan for Venice-of-America had not made adequate provisions for maintenance of the canals.

Chuck Clifton found creative ways to bring in money. He did anything he could for a dollar. He would fish by himself or sometimes he would find jobs on the fishing fleets at the Santa Monica Pier. He began as a deckhand. In time, he was able to graduate from Venice High School, through a continuation program which let him work during the day.

About two weeks after the conversation with the Cliftons on my patio, Charlie called me. He had thought more about his dad and growing up in Venice. He felt that it was important to understand that Chuck not only had economic struggles, but social as well. Venice has been a tricky place for some kids to live for a long time. Charlie told me this story.

It had been a long time ago when Chuck shared this story with him, and he may only have ever shared it once. It seems that during Chuck's teens, there was a roving gang of rough white thugs who called themselves, "The Forty Thieves." They roamed the streets of Venice terrorizing younger kids. Their trick was to find a youth who was alone. Once isolated, and away from would-be rescuers, they would rob their victim of his clothes. Money was so scarce at Chuck's house, that he could not afford to have his cardboard-stuffed shoes stolen. He steered clear of where that gang operated. He confessed to his boys later in life, that it was rough living in Venice when he was growing up. Perhaps adversity during the growing up years has strengthened all of us.

Chuck Clifton career fisherman Santa Monica

A Career Fisherman

By the time Chuck was 20, in 1932, he discovered that if he and his partner fished all the way out at the Ventura County Line, they could catch more fish. They hauled their skiffs up there in a truck and left them there all summer. Chuck used a long line which was about a mile long. He would weigh down both ends with rocks, using floats to keep track of the line. They baited up the line with sardines. When it was full of fish, he and his partner would haul it in, and fill their barrels with the catch. Once on shore, they had the job of getting the barrels onto the beach where they had constructed a wooden slide track. The men would push the heavy barrels up the 45-degree grade. Once loaded onto the truck, they drove them back to the Santa Monica Fish Market. It was a very demanding way to make money.

As he got older, he would captain boats. As Captain of the Scotty in the 1950's, he provided live bait to the sport fishing fleet in the Santa Monica Bay. The photo shows the boat, "Scotty," filled with

Chuck Clifton and his partner pushing barrels of fish uphill.

12 tons of sardines. Chuck is at the stern of the boat. After they sold all the bait, they would head back to the Santa Monica Pier and unload their nets. They would drag them over to the Casino parking lot of the Ocean Park Pier, where they stretched them out for repairs. A fisherman's life was hard. It included backbreaking work; the labor of the catch, plus the effort to sell it. In addition, fishermen had the constant task of keeping up the equipment.

Chuck found other imaginative ways to earn money. One of the most outlandish was as a stunt man. During Abbot Kinney's heydays at the Venice and Ocean Park Pier (also known as Pickering Pier), the promoters hired biplanes to buzz the tourists at the end of the pier. The biplanes were stored off Washington Boulevard in the wetlands acreage which one day would be the Marina del Rey.

Chuck Clifton's bait boat - 12 tons sardines. Chuck at stern of the boat

The more outrageous the biplane antics, the better the crowds liked it. Chuck earned extra money by walking out on the wings of the plane while it was dipping at the end of the pier. Newspaper reports state that Sunday crowds of some 60,000 would witness the antics from Pickering's Pier. I can just imagine the screams from the guests as they watched a young man walking on the wing of the plane as it flew by!

Daring wing walker- Chuck Clifton c 1932

Romance

One day while Chuck was skippering a pleasure fishing boat, he met a young lady named Evelyn Cody. Evelyn was born and raised in Hollywood. She had an older brother, Edwin. The Cody parents rented out rooms. Family lore held that one of their tenants was a bootlegger. Perhaps he helped coordinate the transport of illicit booze to the speakeasies on Windward Avenue?

When Evelyn was in her teens she moved in with relatives. Perhaps the move was to ensure her proximity to her high school, Beverly Hills High School. The family was the Davis family. They were loosely affiliated with the Hollywood scene, as they hosted their own radio show on fishing. Later they took the show to television. For research purposes, the Davises took Evelyn out for a day of pleasure fishing. That trip would change her life. She met the brawny young man, Chuck Clifton.

Their meeting resulted in a romance, marriage, and three children, all of whom would be raised in Venice. The children were Charlyn, and our friends, John and Charlie. Evelyn was the daughter of John

Evelyn and Chuck meet

Pier Café - Blonde woman seated is Marilyn Mills

and Marie Lemmens Cody. Marie Lemmens emigrated from Holland when she was just 18 years-old, speaking no English and having no money. She found her way to Chicago, learned English, and found a job. She met John Cody and moved to California.

John and Marie owned and operated The Pier Café at 2809 Ocean Front Walk, Ocean Park, in the late 1930's into the 1940's. This café was across the boardwalk from the children's park where Jackie and I often played. I'm certain that my family stopped into the cafe for turkey sandwiches. Charlie held up a photo of his Cody grandparents behind the counter of their café. Seated with dark glasses is their mother's cousin, actress Marilyn Mills. Charlie showed me a playbill of a movie starring Marilyn Mills opposite Gary Cooper. Surely, the photo was taken that day to record Marilyn's presence at the diner.

Evelyn and Chuck settled into married life, bought a home just east of Lincoln Boulevard where they raised their family. Evelyn enjoyed a thirty-year career at Paper Mate Pens in Santa Monica. They provided for Chuck's mom, Nellie, all her life. She lived in a granny flat on the back of their property.

With her Grandpa Cody by the Pier Café 1940 – Ocean Park

Lost at Sea

A terrifying adventure befell Chuck. It was probably in the 1940's. He was lost at sea with 35 passengers on board his pleasure fishing boat "Dispatch." Late in the day, when it was time to turn back toward the harbor, the propeller on the boat broke. Communication was by Morse Code over shortwave radio. The seas picked up. Finally, help came in the form of another boat, the fishing boat "Indiana." The "Indiana" tied a tow rope to the "Dispatch." When it began the tow, the rope snapped. They tried again. The wind was seriously picking up. Fearing catastrophe in the high seas, the "Indiana" left them. John remembers this story told by his dad so well that he could almost hear the tap tap tap of Morse code as his father frantically signaled for help. It must have been terrifying. Chuck put out a sea anchor and prepared to protect his passengers until help could arrive. I am sure they all did a lot of praying. They were out there, lost at sea, for three days.

Chuck Clifton professional fisherman

Charlie and John - Growing Up Venice

When the story of their parents and grandparents in Venice concluded, John and Charlie regaled me with their own adventures. The boys attended Venice schools: St. Mark's School for elementary, Mark Twain Junior High, and Venice High School. Charlie spent two years at Santa Monica City College. It was Charlie, taking after his dad, who had a passion for fishing.

As kids, both boys fished. I told you about their very best customers in Chapter Four, the Jewish senior citizens along the boardwalk who kept them in nickels. Remember that sometimes Charlie would go out on the half day boat and would often sell out his catch as the seniors came by? One time he caught a barracuda and got seventy-five cents for it. He reported that he nearly swooned with that kind of money! The old folks would buy out his catches. He has fond memories of selling fish to them.

The boys also collected bottles; two cents for the little ones and five cents for a big one. Both had paper routes. Charlie laughs now as he recalls his very early Sunday morning spiel as he tromped along the pedestrian walkways shouting out *"Examiner Times, Sunday Morning Paper! Examiner Times Sunday morning paper!"* He laughs because he can't believe that the residents just came out and paid him. No one yelled at him for waking them up.

The paper route job required daily folding of papers. Some of the routes were less friendly than others. John explained, "We had to deal with some scary stuff." Their delivery route included the Lincoln Apartments which were known as "Ghost Town." It was a rough neighborhood near Electric and West Washington Boulevard. They had to watch their backs, and bike fast!

My siblings had similar experiences with the same Oakwood area. After my sister, Jackie and I were grown and off to college, our father remarried and had a second family. We have five younger siblings who also grew up in Venice. They went to school with Oakwood kids during the mid-70's and 80's. My brother, Chuck, recalls that by the time they were in school, "it was truly awful." There was a lot of bullying, gang violence, and regular Saturday night shootings. My younger sister, Diana, reports that by the early 1980's, the drug dealers would shoot out the streetlights, so that it was always dark. She hated having to drive home through the area on West Washington Boulevard, now Abbot Kinney Boulevard. It was frightening.

Young John Clifton first paper route

When John was 14-years-old, he got a job working at the Ocean Park Pier which had been refurbished and reopened in 1958 as Pacific Ocean Park, or P.O.P. John worked evenings and after school at a fish stand in front of P.O.P. on the east side of the boardwalk. During the wintertime it got dark early and the area was often a bit deserted. Some tough older guys would come around and demand a serving of shrimp and pickles. John would package it up and ask for payment. There was one guy who refused. That happened repeatedly. John knew he'd lose in a fight, he was so much younger. To get even, one night he urinated all over the pickles. The bully came by. "Gimme a plate of shrimp and pickles!" he demanded. John dished up the food and asked for payment. As usual the tough guy refused. John smiled to himself as the guy sauntered off, biting off a chunk of urine-soaked pickle!

Surfing

As teens, John and Charlie discovered surfing. It became their passion. "We ruled the section of ocean north of P.O.P.," declared John with a big smile. When John and Charlie were not hanging out with their surfing club friends, or surfing the mouth of Ballona Creek, they were in the waves on the north side of P.O.P. by the Tiki Village. Inspired by the kids diving for money off the steamer at Avalon, they called up to the tourists to throw coins. A shower of nickels, dimes and quarters would rain down on them. They delighted the tourists by diving for those coins.

"Mud Lake" known in earlier times as "Ballona Lake" or "Lake Los Angeles" was situated in the wetlands over by where Hoppyland had been. The boys would swim in it. When John was 13 years-old he met his future wife, Sherry South, while swimming there. Sherry's parents moved to Venice in 1936 from Oregon. Her father owned the gas station at the corner of Clune and Washington Boulevard. He joined the Los Angeles Police Department and worked out of the Venice Substation. After he retired from the police force he worked in the film studios as a "grip." When that job ran its course, he opened another gas station across from the market in the Triangle in Culver City. Sherry's mom was a homemaker. John reports that her mother was "very protective of Sherry." It took a few years for her to warm up to John.

Sherry was as excited about surfing as was John. After a while, as they dated, they became a part of the "P.O.P. pier crowd." Pacific Ocean Park, POP, only lasted about ten years before it, too, burned down and was dismantled. It was long enough for their romance to bloom.

Happily, their love has continued throughout their lives. Both are quick to agree that swimming in "Mud Lake" was pretty disgusting! John and Sherry spent a lot of time together

John and Sherry Clifton heading for a day of surfing

exploring Venice as young teens. John remembers bicycling home from Sherry's house on Clune Avenue, just off Washington Boulevard. It would be dark, as he pumped his way home, and he would hear eerie sounds coming from the mostly vacant acreage across Washington Boulevard. It was the shrill wailing sound of a lone bagpipe crying into the night outside of Hoppyland.

John and Sherry married in 1965. John and Charlie went into business together and owned and operated a successful construction company. They worked hard across their lives. Both are proud of their fifty-plus year-long marriages, and their families. Charlie married NyAnn Griess in Venice in 1970. NyAnn and Charlie have lived in their house on Rose Avenue just two blocks past the Venice border for the past fifty years.

Nowadays, John belongs to a paddleboard club made up of old time surfers. He regularly paddleboards around Dana Point Harbor. Charlie still loves surfing. His favorite spot is El Porto in Manhattan Beach.

Growing up Venice for these men has meant a lifetime of good work, casual living, great families, close relationships, and a love affair with the surf and sand.

Charlie Clifton pictured here. Charlie and John enjoyed surfing near Pacific Ocean Park Pier

Snapshot of Pioneers

The day after our interview, I woke up thinking about early California, the Clifton family, and the broader picture of the settling of Los Angeles. I thought about the faces of California; the influence of the Indigenous People, the heritage of the Spanish colonizers, the impact of the Mexican era, the struggle of the Russian Jews escaping the Bolsheviks, the trials of Holocaust survivors, the Japanese farmers, the Chinese workers laying down railroad tracks, and the Europeans who migrated westward from the East. These are just some of the early faces that make up the diverse culture which is Southern California. I thought of my classrooms in the late 60's full of Vietnamese refugees; how they escaped the fall of Saigon and settled in Orange County. The list goes on.

I realize that I have been blessed with a front row seat in the drama of the creation of Southern California. My interview with the Clifton brothers was just a single look at a Venice family. We could look at my family, or we could look at any number of random families, and have a snapshot of what constitutes our city, our state, our nation. All of us are immigrants and have a story.

I thought back to the early weeks of this project when I was sifting through old family documents. Back when I was thinking about taking this project on, I enlisted my siblings to share their memories. Within a day, my brother, Chuck discovered, that he too, held a box of memorabilia. He rifled through it for me, looking for more Venice photos of old. He was quite surprised when he stumbled upon the original 1879 marriage certificate of our great grandparents!

Within minutes, Chuck texted a photo of the certificate to me. I think we were both a bit stunned to discover such a document. Those great grandparents arrived in Los Angeles in the late 1880's, with two small children, and established pharmacies. They both were pharmacists. I marvel that California and its settling is so young; our history is so new, that historical documents are often stuffed in boxes in our attics!

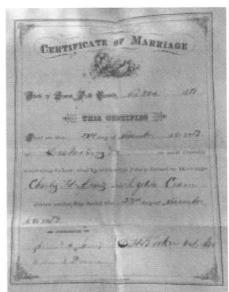

1878 Original Certificate of Marriage

I am grateful to be a part of the colorful story that is California's. This book happens to take a look at Venice, California, but we could start anywhere and we could glimpse a similar, vibrant, interesting portrait of hardworking American pioneers.

John and Charlie sent me some contemporary photos showing their love of the ocean.

John above and Charlie surfing

Charlie and John love the water 2020

Chapter Eight

Surf, Store, Beats, & Music

"Barefoot on the beach, I am happy." Yanni

"May I help you?"

Entering the 1950's, life seemed to swirl around my sister and me. Our grandfather was beginning to slow down. He moved his booming Hollywood store at Sunset and Gardner, to a much smaller storefront on West Washington Boulevard [which today is Abbot Kinney Boulevard] in Venice. It was in a two block commercial district, three blocks in from the traffic circle in downtown Venice; the traffic circle having been Kinney's lagoon.

In 1951, when I was eight, our mother was hired by the Los Angeles Department of Parks and Recreation as a Play Leader at Roosevelt Park in South Central Los Angeles. With our mother no longer at the beach playground, Jackie and I needed to walk to our grandfather's drug store after school. We took this responsibility very seriously as it required a long two-mile walk across busy streets. Sometimes we took a short-cut through the canals. We never ran into trouble, nor felt particularly scared. We were just very serious.

We spent a lot of great times at the drug store. We were wild for the delicious grilled cheese sandwiches made by the owner in the diner next door. Our grandfather would give us

R.W. Lewis, Sr. at Venice Pharmacy 1950

coins and we would slip next door to Manny-the-cook, who would fry them up for us. They were crisp and gooey. We'd race back to our special rocking chair in the backroom and devour them.

Now, as a grandmother, I realize that two little blonde girls standing on tiptoes ordering grilled cheese, or running down the street, must have been charming. All the shopkeepers knew us and chatted with us. We had the run of the entire block and were welcome in all the stores. The business on the other side of the drug store was a market. We were in and out of there all the time for sodas and chips. When Ken and I visited the area a few weeks ago, I was delighted to find that the store fronts were still there, sporting fresh paint, and even the market was still there. It is a liquor store now.

As children Donna and Jackie had the run of the block. Photo May 2020

By the time I was ten, my grandfather decided that I was old enough to wait on customers! Well, that was the most frightening idea he ever had! One day I resolved to meet his challenge. I wore a nice dress and psyched myself into it. I had practiced saying, "May I help you?" all morning. My hands were

Donna in front of W. Washington Pharmacy, 1950

sweaty, and my heart was pumping. I recall that a sweet looking lady came in the front door and was browsing near the cosmetics. I aimed toward her, but fear gripped me, and I chickened out. I sneaked back into the storeroom. My grandfather, observing my dilemma, stepped in. After a bit, I calmed myself down and inhaled a deep breath. It took a few more tries, by the end of the day, I was able to ask if I could help them. Whew. It was smooth sailing after that. I even learned how to use the cash register. Mind you though, it started out being very scary.

My favorite activity at the drug store was to sit on the floor next to the magazine and book rack. My job was to unpack the items and arrange them for display. There were comics which marginally held my interest, but there were *also* some more scientific kinds of magazines. One in particular intrigued me. It was about psychosomatic

108

Donna and Jackie enjoyed run of the block on W. Washington Blvd. now Abbot Kinney Blvd. pic 2020

illnesses. I had to look up some of the words, but it was one publication I looked forward to each month. Jackie and I also played with our storybook dolls in the back room. I liked going to the store and being with our grandfather. The store was not busy all the time, so he had time to teach us about mixing medicines and weighing them out on his shiny brass scales.

Looking back, it seems like we had a chance to learn a lot from him. He never raised his voice; he was generous with his time, money, and candy. Thinking about it now, I realize it was a very enriching way to grow up. Both of our grandparents were always teaching us things.

Surf Riding Mania

The next year, Jackie and I were thrilled when our parents announced that they had purchased a house in Culver City. We would have our own bedroom to share! The beach cottage only offered bunk beds, set behind a screen dividing the living area. This was exciting news!

We started a new school. For me, it was the fourth grade and I met my best friend Leanne. We are still very close, living near one another. Those elementary years went by with a lot of time spent with our grandparents. After we moved out of the cottage, they started using it on weekends.

We began to have more autonomy, even learning how to ride the public bus that serviced Venice Boulevard. We rode the bus to shop at the smart new Culver Center. By the time I was twelve we were allowed to ride it to the beach.

Every weekday during the summer, after we completed our chores, we put our bathing suits on under our clothes and walked to the bus at Venice and Sawtelle Boulevards. We toted our blow-up, blue canvas surf mats with us. We got off at the Santa Monica Pier, and made our way to the south side of the pier where we set up our towels.

We learned to surf on those canvas mats, the precursor to boogie boards. We could catch almost any kind of wave. The waves rolled in a long way. We had great rides. We would stay out in the surf until our fingers were wrinkled and our lips turned blue. We were crazy about surf riding. When we were finally shivering too much, we would leave the waves and go into shore in search of food. Our favorite was the Hot Dog-on-a-Stick stand. It was the first one, the beginning of a popular chain which has stores in many malls to this day. We would gobble up our corn dogs and enjoy the fresh cold lemonade.

Donna still loves surfing - boogey board style. Photo June 2020. San Clemente.

Our exhilarating days in the surf concluded when our dad picked us up after his workday at Douglas Aircraft. By this time, he had risen in his profession, to aerospace designer. Even though we no longer lived on the beach, we found our way back to it. We were in the water almost every non-school day. We were passionate about our surf riding!

Back to 4411 Ocean Front Walk

The State of California had long been making plans to build a freeway which would extend all the way from Santa Monica to Huntington Beach. It would be called the San Diego Freeway, Interstate 405, and ultimately, someday, it would reach to San Diego. Our house at Sawtelle and Braddock Drive was in its path. The State of California, using its powers of eminent domain, negotiated a purchase from our family. I think they paid our parents $12,000. We moved back to the beach house. Our grandparents had added a nice sunroom to it. They postponed using the cottage until our father could build us our own house. This would happen in 1959.

The summer of 1956, when I was fourteen years old, would be a time-dividing summer for me. My friend Leanne and I were staying with her parents' friends in Palos Verdes when I met a boy. He turned my world upside down just by meeting him. I was so stricken that I could not eat nor sleep for the five-day visit. Back at home in Venice, thick special delivery letters from him began to drop through the mail slot in the door of the beach cottage. Those letters came for years. We couldn't drive. Certainly, we were far too shy to talk on the phone. One day in the future I would marry him. His name was Ken Friess. All those thick letters are in a bundle in my cabinet with a ribbon wrapped around them. Perhaps someday my great grandchildren will enjoy reading them.

Ken Friess about age 15

Venice High School

I enrolled in Venice High School in 1957 as a 10th grader. It took a lot of persuasion on my part because our parents' plan was that Jackie and I would attend Santa Monica High School. They believed that Venice High was too "rough," and they did not want us there. Having divorced, our mother rented an apartment overlooking the ocean at the beach near the Del Mar Club in Santa Monica. That qualified us to attend Santa Monica High School, but all my friends from elementary and junior high were going to Venice High School. I negotiated a deal. I convinced my father that I should go to Venice, but only until Jackie was ready for Santa Monica. Thus, I enjoyed a year and a half with my friends.

Donna Lewis age 15 Venice High

I was able to qualify for my driver's license early, when I was fifteen and a half. I felt very grown up because I was the first one in my friend group to drive. One of the most interesting things about Venice High School, besides the big statue of movie star Myrna Loy out in front, was the parking. The Red Car electric train had run down the middle of Venice Boulevard for decades, from downtown Los Angeles, taking beachgoers to the seashore. Once the Red Car public transportation system was abandoned, the tracks remained in the center of the street. They were elevated about six feet with dirt berms up to them; perfect parking lots for students. When it rained, we had fun driving through the puddles, splashing mud everywhere. Once, I got caught up in the wet mud and my car did a 360! My friend, Leanne, was in the car with me.

When we stopped the spinning, we both looked at each other with alarm in our eyes. Neither of us had known what we didn't know about slippery streets and spinning cars. We didn't try that again.

I thrived at Venice High School. My friends were fun and my classes were wonderful. I was not allowed to attend any school events due to my parents' concern about the people at school. Interestingly, my experience did not support their fears. I was in college prep classes. My teachers were top notch. I was performing science experiments at home with nutrient agar and Petri dishes, creating colonies of bacteria. I was held in thrall by all that I was learning. The classes were hard; serious-minded English teachers demanding our best; fascinating content in the science classes. I was inspired and transformed from an average student to an A student.

My college bound classmates seemed as serious as I was. In my drama class, for example, we acted out scenes, practicing after school in some of the students' homes. Even though it was only high school, we cared to work hard. I remember the cast gathering to practice for a play, in our classmate, Beau Bridges' home. He was one year ahead of me. I was in a romantic scene with him, much to the great dismay of the other girls. They were so jealous about it! The scene demanded that he kiss me. He was

From Left: Donna, Jackie and Leanne Godfrey c. 1957

112

the son of the movie star, Lloyd Bridges who, at that time, was starring in the prime-time television series, *Sea Hunt.* That show ran from 1958-1961. Beau was a big deal, and by far the best actor in the class, but he never showed off or acted superior to the rest of us. I felt privileged to have an important scene with him.

Across my life, Golden Globe winner, Beau and his younger brother, Academy Award Best Actor Jeff Bridges, would entertain world-wide audiences. They reminded me of the fine education I received at Venice High School. Even as recently as 2013-2015, I admired my old classmate, Beau and his co-stars in the sitcom, *The Millers*, shown on CBS. Coincidentally, it ran at the same time as another of my classmates, Swoozi Kurtz. Swoozi was in my drama classes at USC. At this writing she has a nice role in the TV series, *Man with a Plan,* starring Matt LaBlanc from *Friends* fame. What has stayed with me across all these years is how down-to-earth those students were, and how graciously they interacted with their fellow classmates.

As inspiring as the Venice High School classroom situation was, life on the black top in gym class was the opposite. I had to learn to stick up for myself. The girls I spent time with were not in my PE class. I'll never forget the day the teacher put us into teams for volleyball. During one of the games, a girl was cheating. She was a pretty girl with penciled-in arches over her plucked-out eyebrows. I knew she was *tough.* The other girls on her side of the net seemed to be her friends. She was cheating with the score. I called her on it. She threatened me and feigned pulling a knife out of her hair. The situation was intimidating, but I stood my ground even though I felt nervous. I was not sure if perhaps she *did* have a knife in her hair. After a few hot exchanges she backed down. Later, the girls on my team said they were afraid that I was going to fight with her. *Fight?* I'd never fought in my

Storefront 52 Brooks Avenue, a block up from the boardwalk

life. That tense interaction gave me a new confidence I'd never before felt. A few days after that, at home, my parents caught me plucking out my eyebrows. They had a *fit*. My eyebrows never really did grow back. It's funny. I didn't like that girl. Why would I pluck my eyebrows?

House Construction 2909 Ocean Front Walk

At about this time, our father purchased a vacant lot at 2909 Ocean Front Walk and proceeded to have us girls help him build our new house. I know it built character, because every single day, Jackie and I walked from 4411 to 2909 and moved sand. That's right! We were tasked with the job of moving a huge sand dune on the front of the lot to the back of it. I suspect now that our father was simply ensuring that we stayed out of trouble. We started this project in the summer before I could drive, probably in 1956.

The lot had six concrete pilings at the front where its former house had been. I saw a photo taken from 25th street looking north in the 1940's, the beach was eroded to the actual wooden boardwalk. I can imagine the devastating storm damage to those houses. Anyway, we were happy that we were not assigned the job of jack hammering the pilings out! We knew that several houses along that part of the beach, up from 2909 had been "washed away," meaning that there had been great storm damage. Our property was bordered by a wide wooden planked boardwalk. The walk included a wood hand railing and the walk itself was a bit elevated. One had to take three steps to get up on it. I vividly recall the locals out for their morning walks. They loved to stop and lean on that railing, looking down on our project. They were never in a hurry and enjoyed striking up conversations with us. I thought their time would have been better spent by grabbing a shovel and helping out. We filled countless wheelbarrows with sand that summer and got to know our neighbors. By the time school started I was horrified to discover definition in my biceps. It was not a look I was trying for! It took us about two years to complete the house.

52 Brooks Avenue Parallel Universes

In 1958, our grandfather decided to retire to spend his time playing checkers with his pals. Our entrepreneurial father saw this as an opportunity to provide my sister and me with a real-life learning opportunity, while unloading the remainder of the pharmacy's nonprescription stock. While our classmates practiced business skills in a make-believe world a Junior Achievement Program at school, our father rented another storefront at 52 Brooks Avenue at the corner of Pacific, one block up from the beach. He set us up with counters, the old cash register, cosmetics stock, magazines and sundries. With the new driver's license in my pocket, Jackie and I were dispatched to the Smart and Final Wholesale store on Rose Avenue where we loaded up on soft drinks, snacks and candies to sell to our customers.

We negotiated with Kodak Film and were a photo drop off site. We were in business.

Each school day, I picked Jackie up from Palms Junior High School. We opened the store about 3:30 p.m. on weekdays and closed at 8:00 p.m. On Saturdays we were open from 10-6. It was a remarkable way to get to know the neighborhood, while learning how to run an actual business. We kept the soft drinks in a big red cooler that said *Coca Cola – Ice Cold* on its side. All the drinks were submerged in cold water, a sliding lid moved to one side. It was our responsibility to maintain the water at a cold temperature. Friendly Venetians stopped in for snacks and sodas. They would talk to us in the casual way of customers. They were a mixed bag of people, all ages, probably lower middle-income levels, and mostly white.

Through the store, we felt comfortable with the locals, but sometimes in the winter, when it was dark outside, we knew that passers-by could see us, two young girls, in the lighted store. Occasionally, that feeling creeped us out. We never let our guard down, though no one ever really bothered us. Maybe a little bit. I learned to put a hard edge to my voice if some weird guy got overly sociable. A drunk

Sundry Store Staff: Jackie left, age 13, Donna age 15

person now and again would stumble in, but we handled them, and got on with doing our homework. We both kept up straight A's. There was no time for goofing off.

In the fall of 1959, Jackie and I both transferred to Santa Monica High School. I was fine about the change because my best friend, Leanne, was also leaving Venice High School. Jackie wanted to attend there, and I was her ride. We continued to operate our store. Sometimes Ken would stop by the store on his way to surf at County Line. We liked each other. We smiled and flirted. Sometimes we went out on dates, but he lived twenty-five miles away in Rolling Hills, and clearly, I was busy most of the time.

Beatniks at the Gas House

About a year into our store operation, a different sort of folk began to filter by our window. They were not the neighborhood regulars. They were artists, performers, poets, and writers, heading to the popular Gas House which opened in 1959. It was just down the street from us at 1501 Ocean Front Walk. In the decades to come it would become legendary, associated with a movement which has had a lasting impact on American literature.

Hippies invade Venice c. 1960's Photo Licensed by Shutterstock

Enthusiastic patrons of the Gas House might have been going to perform dramas, to read poetry, or talk smack about contemporary "cookie cutter American suburbia." Their philosophy was seen by mainstream American culture as a counter-culture. They were dubbed "Beatniks," a term they despised. The adjective "beat" seems to have come from their rejection of the typical 8-5 workers' lives. Their philosophy implied that middle class housewives and their fedora-wearing husbands were "beat" from their "meaningless toils."

The use of the term, "nik," came along with the 1957 launching of the Russian's "Sputnik, the world's first satellite orbiting the Earth. It was a negative reference, loosely associating them with Russians. For ordinary American society, the term "Beatnik" represented a negative image. Society didn't approve of their drugs, free sex, or criminal activity.

The Beat Generation visited Venice coffee houses – shared poetry

The Beat Generation rejected materialism as it ushered in new forms of music, literature and art. It was predominately a literary movement but influenced music as well as art. It began when certain World War II soldiers returned home from war, filled with disillusionment, and searching for meaning. They were writers. Many took up residence in Venice because the rents were low. They also gravitated to the low-rent areas of San Francisco's North Beach, and New York City's Greenwich Village. As the movement gained traction, writers such as Allen Ginsberg, Jack Kerouac, and poet, Lawrence Ferlingetti added gravitas.

The Beat Movement strummed along during the long years of the Cold War which lasted from 1947 through 1991. The Hippie Movement of the 1960's descended from this counterculture. Some of the Beat's key players, adapted to the Hippie vibe and celebrated Love-Ins and the Flower Child philosophy. The unpopularity of the Vietnam War empowered the Flower Children and gave them more social traction. During this long era, a great majority of Americans were highly fearful of Russia and Communism. This viewpoint forced the Beat and Hippie cultures to the fringes of society.

The Beats – Photo licensed Shutterstock

A Culture of Non-conformity

The non-conforming ethos of these Beat writers has had a lasting impact upon the broader social and political culture of America. By 1969, for instance, I was firmly established at Cypress College as a full time English teacher. I particularly enjoyed teaching the unconventional poetry of Lawrence Ferlingetti. His work had made its way into our class anthology. My students were crazy about his vivid images and his lack of punctuation. His poetry excited them.

Professor Donna, Cypress College
c. 1968

One poem in particular, really set their imaginations on fire! It was in "The World is a Beautiful Place," where he used an image of a person going around "goosing statues." A few years forward, as my classes began to fill with Vietnam veterans, the enthusiasm level in my students for the rebelliousness of some of the "Beat" work, such as Jack Kerouac's *On the Road* grew further. Of course, by today's standards, the literature of the Beat Generation has become mainstream.

Here is one of my all time favorite Beat poems. This is Lawrence Ferlingetti's 1955 works: "The world is a beautiful place." [Note he did not use conventional stylistic devices such as punctuation or capitalization.]

> **The world is a beautiful place**
> **to be born into**
> **if you don't mind happiness**
> **not always being**
> **so very**
> **much fun**
> **if you don't mind a touch of hell**
> **now and then**
> **just when everything is fine**
> **because even**
> **in heaven**
> **they don't sing**
> **all the time**

The world is a beautiful place
           to be born into

if you don't mind some people dying
           all the time
    or maybe only starving
           some of the
time
  which isn't half so bad
           if it isn't you
Oh the world is a beautiful place
           To be born into
   if you don't much mind
           a few dead minds
  in the higher places
           or a bomb or two
  now and then
           in your upturned
faces
  or such improprieties
           as our Name Brand
society
    in prey to
           with the men of
distinction
  and its men of extinction
           and its priests
   and other patrolmen
           and its various
segregations
  and congressional investigations
           and other
constipations
    that our fool flesh
           is heir to

The Gas House was just down from 52 Brooks. It was only open for three years but had a lasting impact on the character of Venice.

Yes, the world is the best place of all
For a lot of such
things as
making the fun scene
and making the love
scene
and making the sad scene
and singing love songs of
having

inspirations

and walking around
looking at everything
and smelling
flowers
and goosing statures
and even thinking
and kissing
and making babies and wearing pants
and wearing hats
and dancing
and
going swimming
in rivers
on picnics
in the middle of the
summer
and just generally
"living it up"
Yes
But there right in the middle of it
Comes the smiling
mortician

The Beats Were Innovators

By the late 1950's the Beat's soul-searching philosophy attracted like-minded people who could be found in jazz clubs, enjoying the cool jazz sounds of saxophonist Charlie Parker, and the harmonic notes of trumpeters Dizzy Gillespie and Miles Davis. Authors, Jack Kerouac and Allen Ginsberg were also frequent visitors to such clubs of New York City. These jazz players, and song composers added layers of sound, in ways previously unheard. They were innovators. Their creative ideas greatly influenced up-and-coming musicians such as Pink Floyd, The Beatles, and Bob Dylan. Not only were their writing styles and musical scores influencers, so was their "look." It became "hip" to emulate the jazz folk by wearing berets and sunglasses and growing goatees. If you look at the "hipster" scene today, you will see parallels.

In later years, Jack Kerouac would describe the "Beat Generation" as *"a generation of crazy, illuminated hipsters suddenly rising and roaming America, serious, bumming, and hitchhiking everywhere, ragged, beatific, beautiful in an ugly, new graceful way."*

The same was true for the Hippies of the 1960's.

Back at 52 Brooks Avenue

Back at 52 Brooks Avenue, my sister and I continued to take notice of the crowd strolling by in the early evening toward The Gas House. There were more beret-wearing men going by than women. Sometimes a woman dressed in a long flowing skirt would catch our eye, but it seemed like more men. We were not frightened, but we were highly aware of our differences. I felt decidedly uncool in my school-girl clothes with my classroom books spread out in front of me.

It was an education watching them meander by, knowing that something big was going on culturally and that we were in no way a part of it, would never be a part of it. I couldn't wrap 'The Establishment" around myself fast enough. We were bookish students

Venice was one of three important Beat Generation gathering spots in the United States. North Beach in the Bay Area, Greenwich Village in NYC, and Venice. 1950'[s.

121

and understood what counterculture meant. We knew there were drugs and free love, none of which were for us.

The Gas House was only open for three years, but it had a big impact on the reputation of Venice. It attracted other like-minded people. Venice became one of the few hot spots in the country for the Beats of the late 50's and early 60's. As the anti-war protesters began to organize and the Hippie Movement grew, Venice was a logical gathering point. My studies show that the established neighbors in Venice were none too happy with the new arrivals.

Donna as Rec Leader LA Dept Parks and Recreation 1960

My sister and I kept our distance, but we were keen observers. Sometimes, while it was still light outside, we would walk by the Gas House and look in. The people seemed like "characters" to us, people from novels. The irony is that in the decades to follow, those people *would* become characters in the writings of others, and some would become famous for the characters in *their* own novels. For us, they just looked like they were in costume.

I graduated from Santa Monica High School in June of 1960 and began classes at Santa Monica City College. At that point, our father closed down the store. We had done a fine job of selling off the stock. I became a Recreation Leader for the Los Angeles Department of Parks and Recreation where I worked after school. Jackie continued at Santa Monica High School, and needing to help out financially, she found an after-school job at the brand new and exciting Pacific Ocean Park.

Ken and Donna photo booth at POP 1960

Donna and Ken continued to see one another 1962

Chapter Nine

Venice Beach a Mecca for Creative Artists

*"All the knowledge I possess everyone else can acquire, but my heart
is exclusively my own." Goethe (1740-1832)*

The Beat Generation set the scene for Venice to become iconic in new, creative ways. Today's Venice is an enclave for artists, musicians, creative graffitists, muralists, and performance artists. Television and movie producers rely on the intrigues of the boardwalk and canals for shooting scenes. Murals cover the walls and buildings with stunning public art. Musicians can be heard strumming new riffs as one walks down the Speedway. Venice offers a thousand flavors.

I laughed to myself thinking about the *flavors* of Venice, and my friend, Christine's astonishment when I told her the topic of this book. She had exclaimed, "Oh my gosh! I once visited there. It was in 1982. I walked around the boardwalk with my eyes and mouth wide open. There were so many unusual

Mural on the back of Windward Ave building –
Reminder of early Hotel St. Marks on Windward.
Photo May 2020.

Mural on the back of 52 Brooks Avenue

sights and people. One woman, a very big person, zoomed by me on roller skates. She had long purple hair flowing about. At first I thought she was naked! I worried, but finally I could see bits of bikini." Chuckling as she settled into her memory, she added, "The highlight of the day was seeing ten rainbow kites flying in formation. I was so fascinated that I went up to the man flying them. He offered to let me try, but the wind was too strong, he had to help me. Together we flew some loops. It was exhilarating! I've never forgotten that day at Venice Beach."

Memorial mural to honor basketball legend Kobe Bryant

This singing skating entertainer has been on the boardwalk for at least 20 years.

Jackie and I have a younger half-sister who grew up seven years behind me. She is Dee Dee Lewis Keel. As a girl she was fascinated by anything celebrity. From her early teen years, she studied and followed the successes of rock music groups. I remember looking at the walls in her room when she was a young teenager and seeing posters of the Beatles and Rolling Stones. Truly, those groups barely registered on my radar, but they were enchanting to her. She has been a devotee of many such musical greats; and has become something of a lay expert on Rock and Roll music.

I asked her to write an article on her *Growing Up Venice,* as her experience was far different from mine. I think you will find this most fascinating. As this writing project developed, I began to see the beauty and grace with which Venice offers space for multiple parallel universes. Dee Dee was privy to one that I was not. Enjoy her story.

Growing Up Venice
by Dee Dee Lewis Keel

My first memories of growing up in Venice Beach are of playing in the water-flooded alley behind my grandfather's drugstore. It was my 2nd birthday in 1952. I wore a green bathing suit and romped around with such joy. I have vivid memories of two drugstore locations in Venice; one on Washington Blvd (which is now called Abbott Kinney Blvd) and the other on the corner of Brooks Ave. and Pacific Ave. Looking back, I think Venice was a wonderful, eclectic place filled with unusual people which created a colorful, creative culture. As I grew up, I admired the locals who created the wide variety of arts in Venice.

The ocean front, where my family lived, was a place my sisters and I spent much time as little girls. The beaches stretched for miles with a few small houses. Standing tall were oil rigs looking like gigantic soldiers along the coast. The continuous sound of their churning became a symphony which lulled us to sleep at night. The sound of waves crashing onto shore, or the weekly whistle sound of the Helms Bakery truck coming by with fresh donuts, added to the symphony.

In my mind, that was the beginning of the true music scene in Venice Beach. At an early age, I began to be in sync with the rhythms and beats of Venice Beach. This magical place seemed far and away from the busy streets of Los Angeles and I loved it.

Star Struck

At age 11, I became extremely intrigued with Hollywood movie stars. This may be due to both sets of grandparents living in the Hollywood area. My mother and I visited her father often; he had a few failed attempts at becoming an actor. He loved telling tales of Hollywood stars. My father's mother had been on television. The mother of my half sisters, Dorothy Lewis, was a star of the Santa Monica Opera. My half sister, Donna, performed in live stage shows at Santa Monica City College. I was exposed to quite a bit of dazzling showmanship and loved it!

Being that I was my mother's only child at the time, in a way I was an only child. My mother worked long hours, I came home after school to an empty apartment or to a nearby babysitter. My mother and I had moved from Venice to a few different apartments, in nearby Culver City, then to Santa Monica. Watching '60's television shows consumed many hours for me. I began to read movie star magazines and dreamed of meeting the glamorous people depicted in them.

In the summer of 1962, while running on the beach in front of 2909 Ocean Front Walk, my school girlfriend and I ran across the famous actors, Troy Donahue and Suzanne Pleshette. They were sunbathing. We were stunned to see real live movie stars on our beach! The couple was very nice. They allowed us to come in close and say hello. This began my quest to seek out celebrities; to see them "for real" not just on magazine pages.

By early 1963, America was hit by the 'British Invasion' of The Beatles. I was smitten and fell right into the screaming teenage frenzy over-taking girls my age. My father had finally married my mother and we were living full time in Venice Beach. I was enrolled in junior high school at Mark Twain but ended up graduating from Palms Junior High in the last semester. My father had a disagreement with my science teacher and transferred me to Palms. Not knowing any of my classmates, I stayed to myself. One lunch break I noticed a girl showing off photographs of herself with some of the British bands that had followed The Beatles over to America. Her name was Susan and her father was the author Ray Bradbury!

Dee Dee Lewis Mark Twain Jr. High School

The British idols were all coming to her house to meet him. Ray Bradbury was a very famous science fiction author. His novel, Fahrenheit 451, was required reading in most English classes. I spent many lunch breaks listening to Susan's tales of meeting some of my music idols.

The Beatles were coming to the Hollywood Bowl on August 23, 1964. I begged my father to let me go. My prayers were answered when he told me I could, and there were free tickets with box seats! This was made possible because my grandmother, Vera May Lewis, was head of the department in the Los Angeles County Department of Parks and Recreation which handled the Hollywood Bowl! I was beyond excited waiting for the day to come. Box seats for four and all set to go…then the arguing began. No one wanted to take me! My older half-sister, Jackie, was nominated. Jackie brought her best friend. It's funny, to this day she doesn't remember a thing about that night! Our seats were absolutely amazing. When The Beatles finally came out on stage, it was so shocking that I had a hard time believing they were real. I couldn't hear a word they were singing but I didn't care because, "I loved them Yeah, Yeah, Yeah!"

In October 1964 I was eagerly awaiting the arrival and performances of The Rolling Stones.

Being a rebellious 15-year-old, I had switched my allegiance from the clean-cut Beatles to the ruffian look and sound of The Stones. I had secured free tickets to the filming of the T.A.M.I. show [Teen Age Music International] at the Santa Monica Civic Auditorium. The auditorium was just one mile from my home. Free tickets were given out to all of the local schools! The famous singing duo, Jan and Dean, were the hosts of the show. The playbill included some famous British bands, as well as a performance by the legendary James Brown. It was unbelievable to have all of these famous artists right by my home!

In December 1965, The Rolling Stones were scheduled to perform at the Los Angeles Sports Arena. I had met a girl at school who shared my love of the band, and unbelievably, her father was the general manager of the arena ...just how lucky could I be? We were taken to the show by her father and put into incredible seats right up front.

Venice High School

Not long after that amazing concert, I started Venice High School. I loved the history of the beautiful school. The fact that a statue of the glamorous movie star Myrna Loy stood out front was a beacon for me!

By this time, my girlfriend and I were crazy for the band "The Young Rascals." We wrote their names on our notebooks, cut out photos in teen magazines, and each claimed our favorite guy in the band. We thought they looked so cute in the neatly pressed little-school-boy outfits which they wore in promotion photos, and on their album cover.

In January of '66 the band was booked at a fairly new club, the Whisky a Go Go, on the Sunset Strip in Hollywood. At 15 years-old, we knew we were too young to get into the show but that was all we could talk about every day at lunch break. From my desk in history class I could see my friend's tiny tan Volkswagen parked along the center divider on Venice

Dee Dee in plaid jumper with her mom and brother Ray.

Boulevard and my mind was far away from the boring lesson on Germany's entry into World War 1. I was in pure agony and couldn't sit still listening to the teacher's voice droning on and on. As soon as the class bell rang to move onto last period, we grabbed our notebooks, and headed straight across the street and jumped in the car. We quickly sped up Venice Boulevard. I felt a huge sigh of relief as the view of our school became smaller and smaller. We zoomed toward Hollywood.

I had never ditched school or done anything against the rules. If you don't count being sent to the Principal's office for wearing my favorite plaid mini-dress inspired by the '60's Mod Movement. Students weren't allowed to show our knees. My jumper was half-way up my thigh! I loved wearing the styles I saw on the Mod girls in my teen magazines. Other than that incident, I was a model teen in school. I always figured if I just followed the rules nobody would notice if I ran off the rails. Boy I did! As the '60's rolled on and the Hippie movement got stronger, I was bewitched. On that ditch day, we arrived at the Whiskey A Go Go, and just stared straight up at the marquee. Huge red plastic letters spelled out the band's name. It was like a lighthouse beam showing us the way. It was an amazing sight for two young school girls standing on Sunset Boulevard. We stared up in awe.

Celebrity Sighting

It was the summer 1965 when my girlfriend, who lived on Linnie Canal, came to get me. There was a long-haired hippie she wanted to follow around the beach. The guy turned out to be Jim Morrison, the singer in a new band called the Doors, who would one day become an icon in the rock and roll world. Jim was staying in various apartments near the beach. We found him at 1811 Ocean Front Walk and sort of stalked him. He came outside just before sunset and walked the beach wearing only leather pants. Our father told me to "Stay away from that dirty hippie!"...

One day after school, we walked down Pacific Avenue, not far from Washington Boulevard, where a building had been torn down. There was no chain length fence enclosing the area. However, all of the doors from the previous house had been fashioned together to form a fence-like barrier. Those doors even had the old glass doorknobs attached! There was graffiti scrawled across the front

of one that read "The Doors of Perception." We thought that was so profound. Later we were told that Jim Morrison had written it. Not long after that time, the band began performing in Hollywood at the club called London Fog.

Aragon Ballroom

In 1967 the famous Aragon Ballroom located on the Ocean Park Pier became the hip Cheetah Club. In the mid 1950's the Aragon Ballroom was a popular dance arena, made famous, by bandleader Lawrence Welk and his big band, the Champagne Music Makers. Welk and his Music Makers were so popular that The Lawrence Welk Show was a staple of television from 1951 - 1982. The shows were televised on Saturday nights. I can remember many times in my preteens, seeing the champagne bubbles floating from the pier as Lawrence Welk began his shows.

When the Welk show was moved into a Hollywood studio, the Aragon Ballroom went looking for new attractions. At one point in '65-'66 it was transformed into a rollerskating rink hosting Roller Derby. After other failed attempts to keep the Aragon open, it became the Cheetah Club. As the Cheetah Club, the Venice Beach area attracted the Rock and Roll crowd. Headliners included Jim Morrison and The Doors, Alice Cooper, and even early Pink Floyd! Unfortunately, in 1970 The Aragon was destroyed by fire.

At this time, I discovered that the entire Alice Cooper Band was living close-by, in a house on Walgrove Avenue near my junior high school! Imagine that, a real live rock band had been living so close by me for years!

The Cheetah Club was an amazing venue inside and out. My best memory is seeing The Doors performance in '67. Outside, the marquee was high on top of the building front with a giant cutout of a cheetah cat above huge red letters spelling out CHEETAH. Crowds of long-haired guys and girls in fringed leather jackets, large bell bottom pants, and mini dresses hovered around outside, and gathered inside by the stage. While the band played high above the dance floor, psychedelic lights flashed around the room.

Dee Dee Lewis Keel booking groups at the Whiskey

Working at the Whisky A Go Go

Meanwhile, I spent as many days and nights as I could hanging out on the street in front of The Whisky. My father would drive me up and drop me off. He would pick me up before the 10 p.m. curfew. After I got my own car, I was able to go on my own. It was in 1970 when The Whisky owner, Elmer Valentine, saw me. He asked if I would come into the office temporarily to answer phones for a couple of weeks, while he looked for a new secretary. As it turned out I was hired and stayed for nearly 13 years, from 1971-1983. I was finally on the Sunset Strip and in the center of the popular music scene.

While working at The Whisky, I lived in Venice Beach, got married and raised a family. My new husband and I bought a property at 414 Pacific Avenue, at Dudley Avenue, and built a small house. I traveled each day up Venice Boulevard passing by Venice High to work. One day in mid-summer I saw a lot of activity on the campus which was unusual as school was out for the summer. Making my way closer to see what was going on, I discovered a film crew at work. It was the making of the movie *Grease*! John Travolta and Olivia Newton-John were at my alma mater for weeks that summer. I made sure to pass by each day and catch a glimpse...It was very exciting!

We had homes at 4411 and 2909 Ocean Front Walk, which were built by our father. Later, our father purchased an old beach bungalow at 2815 Ocean Front Walk. The house next door to it was huge by comparison. That neighboring house had always fascinated me. It had once belonged to a well-known Hollywood movie producer.

In 1987, Paramount Studios rented our 2815 bungalow to film the movie *Summer School* starring Mark Harmon and Kirstie Alley. It was very exciting to be able to visit a movie set located on our own property.

Growing up in Venice was life-defining for me. The rhythms of the oil wells, the parade of celebrities, and the intrigue of the many different types of people, fascinated me. In my professional life at The Whiskey, many of its musicians frequented Venice Beach. It gave me a common ground with them. Venice had become well known for its hip, cool, and creative culture. It is a part of me, and remains an exciting California attraction to this day.

Dee Dee watched this scene being filmed for Summer School

Following up with Dee Dee

I so appreciated the remarkable accounting which my sister Dee Dee shared regarding her growing up years and her interest in the theater, music, celebrity; all of it. We were chatting and she told me of a time-dividing moment in her young teen years. It had to do with a play I was in at Santa Monica College. I asked her to share it with you.

I've looked up to my sister Donna for as long as I can remember. She has a captivating air about her. Growing up with her was fun and exciting. She always looked just like one of the movie stars in the magazines; I loved to read as a preteen. As I began getting more interested in the arts of our hometown of Venice Beach, there was one single event that cemented my deep love of live performance. Donna was in the cast of a theater production at her school, Santa Monica City College. I didn't know exactly what to expect. In fact, I wasn't thrilled with the idea of going. Little did I know it was to impact me so greatly.

It was springtime and a bit warm out that early evening, as we walked along the street toward the campus theatre. A stretch of fencing at the school was draped with the prettiest sheets of honeysuckle. I remember running my hand across it as we walked by. The sweet scent of it stayed on my hands.

The foyer of the theater had signs and photos of the event that boasted the name of the show. "Clowns Around"...I thought that was silly.

We took our seats and I was immediately drawn in as the actors began taking the stage. I had not seen anything like this; it was as though my movie star magazines had come to life! Suddenly Donna came onto the stage and I was captivated to the point of being frozen in my seat. She was bigger than life and more stunning than usual in her make-up. I was thrilled by her presence and excited that she was my sister and an entire audience was watching her. It was an amazing experience and I carry such fond memories of that evening. To this day, whenever I smell honeysuckle it brings me right back to Donna's night on stage.

Chapter Ten

Venice's Surfing Culture Takes Off

*"Surfing soothes me. The rest of the world disappears for me
when I'm on a wave." Paul Walker*

Surfing at Venice Beach

A bit of research about Venice Beach as a surf spot showed that "Surfing in Venice is good for all levels. It is the place to surf if you want to be seen." The site, *Tourist Attractions in Los Angeles, California* explained that the breakwater is the main Venice surf spot, as well as the end of pier at the end of Washington Boulevard."

My sister, Jackie, and I loved the canvas surf mats of the 1950's, however, in order to catch what we considered to be really great waves, we had to go to the surf next to the Santa Monica Pier. The waves in front of our house broke too close to the beach. They were only good for short body surfing rides. A generation or so later, the technology of surfboards has evolved.

After Jackie and I went off to college, our father finished the construction of his three-story house at 2909 Ocean Front Walk and grew a big second family to fill it. Our second in-line brother, Chuck, an age mate to my son, Rick, became a surfer.

As my friends and family heard more about my Growing Up Venice project, they began to recall their own memories. The texts and emails started to flood in. It seemed a lot of us were excited about Growing Up Venice.

Chuck was intrigued by the surf and became a very accomplished surfer. I have had the pleasure of watching him in the waves. He is graceful and beautiful to watch. I love him very much and he generously wrote about his life growing up on the beach to share with you.

Rick Friess (left) and his uncle Chuck Lewis
Venice Beach c. 1968

"Getting the Stoke"
by Chuck Lewis

The surfing culture in Venice in the late 1970's started really taking off! Before that, I remember lots of body surfing and some board surfing, but it was not as big then. My big bother Ray was a really skilled bodysurfer, like quicksilver on a wave, and truly fearless on big waves. He would take off on these monsters and drop into stand-up sized hollow barrels with crushing thickness (due to the steep beach shelf). You have to experience it to appreciate it.

Ray was fun to watch, but I was often just making sure he came up afterwards! He is still graceful to this day on a wave. Then along came the wide availability of the "Morey Boogie" boards. Suddenly everyone was able to experience something closer to actual surfing. My friends and I quickly moved to boogie boards, and then right through those, to hard boards--we got the stoke.

I started board surfing in Venice around 1977 or 78 on an old Blue Cheer single fin. I found it in the Recycler Magazine and begged my mom to drive me to north Santa Monica, to buy it from an older guy who was done surfing. It was a good-looking board, but really hard to ride. Surfing in Venice was just hard--the waves break super-fast and are mostly what surfers call "close-outs," which are waves that break all at once.

Living beachfront had its perks: My friends and I surfed five to six days a week and it didn't matter what the conditions were, we just wanted to be in the water, anywhere from the Venice fishing pier to Bay Street in Santa Monica.

We learned that the little jetty at the end of Venice Boulevard had a pretty good left or right, depending on the conditions. We got better and better at fast take offs and really quick bottom turns, so we could actually ride the difficult Venice waves.

I remember the first time we hitched a ride from my friend Todd's mom, up to Malibu, we could not believe waves were so easy to catch and ride! We imagined we were in Hawaii because the surfing was so easy. We found we had some serious skills for our ages.

Sometimes, when the conditions were just right in Venice, that little jetty would deliver an amazing wave and suddenly the big boys would show up out of nowhere. This was before the *Surfline* website or cell phones. How they got word out that our little jetty was happening, must have been through good old-fashioned land line calls.

I remember one day we had these big perfect waves and suddenly the world showed up. We had a famous local Venice

Chuck Lewis loves surfing. 2815 Ocean Front Walk, Venice, 1978. Chuck about 14 years old.

136

surfer named Alan Sarlo who showed up with his camera crew, and a bunch of his local buddies. Some were from the Dogtown and Z Boy fame, and suddenly our break was taken over. We were just the little guys. One of those shots from that day made *Surfer Magazine*.

I remember another year when the big breakwater in front of the Venice Pavilion was breaking huge lefts. This was rare, as the tide had to be right for waves that big. You could paddle out in the protection of the big T shaped breakwater and then sneak out between big sets. I was sitting out there on a huge day, watching the big boys dominate these monster lefts, which had these rolling, slow takes offs and really long rides, when suddenly one of the guys pointed at me and told everyone out there that the wave coming was for me.

Nobody challenged him. They all started yelling for me to paddle hard and cheered me on. I caught that wave and rode the longest ride I had ever ridden before, all the way to the inside of the beach to where I had to walk back. I was beyond stoked. I don't know who the guy was, but I've paid it forward a few times since then, for little guys sitting out in the line-up with us.

Venice became a huge cultural center for surfing and skateboarding. We were buying our surfboards and building skateboards from Z-Flex. Its headquarters was a little house on Pacific Avenue. We got to know their pro-riders. As we got older, we often joined them to surf locally and skate. One of nicest guys was Dennis Agnew, aka "Polar Bear,"

Chuck Lewis has been an avid surfer his entire life. This is a recent photo. Chuck takes his family on surf vacations around the world looking for the perfect wave. Photo courtesy of Chuck.

who was a few years older than we. He often let us tag along. I even bought one of his old pro surfboards and rode it to death. The entire scene in the area was amazing. In the early 80's the scene further grew with competitions, skate parks, and lots of people out in the line-ups when the waves were big. It was a great childhood.

A few days after Chuck emailed me his surfing memories, he had more to say. I think he was sitting on his boat at Catalina with lots of time on his hands and his cell phone or laptop at hand. He, like our sister Dee Dee, was interested in the celebrities and the Venice scene. He wanted to share these memories:

Chuck's Childhood Explorations

One of the most memorable experiences for me growing up, was exploring the area from the canals, down all the way down the strand, to Ballona Creek. Back in the early and mid 70's there were no houses on the other side of the canal behind the ABC streets south of Washington Boulevard. [The City of Los Angeles renamed all the streets on the Venice Peninsula, including Nightingale Elementary to Anchorage School.]

We'd take our bikes and explore the oil fields, some with derricks still pumping away, with their signature sound, we all grew up hearing. We'd catch lizards, explore the empty lots, and play on the equipment from the oil fields. We knew where to get a drink of water from hoses behind houses, and how to sneak into the famous Hinanos Bar on Washington Boulevard. We liked their overly salty popcorn.

Nick's Liquor and convenience store at the corner of Washington and Speedway was always an option over going home for food. They had some display shelves opposite the

register where people would drop coins. Sometimes they would lose them. Our small arms and hands could fit under there to gather the coins. Back then, a candy bar was just 11 cents, a quarter was like hitting the jackpot.

We also loved the days in the summer when our grandmother would come down to the beach to spend the day with us. I remember when her huge gold Cadillac would arrive. Somehow, she and our dad, would get it parked about an inch from the wall in our tight driveway. The 2909 house was built on a 28' wide by 90' deep lot, so two side yards and three parking spots in 28 feet made for some serious parking skills.

Our grandmother, Maymie, would take all of us for a long walk down the beach to the pavilion area at Windward Avenue. We

Nick's Market (formerly Tony's) is a staple at the end of Washington Boulevard. Photo June 2020 would swim in the shelter of the break water where little or no waves would bother us. We'd build sandcastles and dig holes to find sand crabs.

As we got older, we also loved exploring the boardwalk action where you could see all kinds of shows during the summer or any weekend. We'd watch chainsaw juggling, fire-eating, roller skate competitions, and more, on the huge concrete pavilion. There was lots of shopping for souvenirs, art, and just about anything else you might want. Venice had something for everyone.

Maymie's Cadillac before it was painted gold.

Celebrities

Venice was always a place to see celebrities, some became even more famous later on. Body builder, movie star, Arnold Swartzenegger was a common sight at the time. We sometimes saw him jogging down the beach in front of our house. We even had one of the Beach Boys, or a close friend of theirs, living in a house behind ours. We got to hear them jamming from time to time.

I had a funny experience with Brian Wilson of the Beach Boys around 1982 late one night. I was leaving the 2909 house with my girlfriend and walking to the 2815 house where I was parked, when Wilson pulls up alongside us and hails us. He tells us that he had just had eye surgery and could not see well. He offered me $100 bucks to drive him home (that was a lot of money back then!).

We were pretty sure his eyes were bloodshot for different reasons, but my girlfriend's mom was super tough on her curfew. If I wanted to keep dating her, I had to get her home on time, so I had to say no. He begged a little, but we had to go, so we let him drive off into the dark. As he made the turn, not-so-well, onto 28th Street, I thought if something happened to him, this would be on me! I was relieved the next day that his name was not in the news. Somehow, he made it home.

Our dad owned a second house a few doors north. He rented the 2815 house to a movie studio in the mid 80s for the filming of *Summer School,* starring Mark Harmon. The house was being sold, so they got to do whatever they wanted to it. They took the little house and transformed it into something much cooler, and hip, to match the surfer teacher character played by the actor Mark Harmon. We enjoyed watching the filming. While it was not, perhaps, the best film, it was super fun watching them make it.

Growing Up Venice offered me a world of experiences I would not have had anyplace else.

Chuck Lewis

Muscle Beach - famous for body builders. June 2020.

Souvenir shops Photo June 2020 – Old Cadillac Hotel building c. 1910.

Boardwalk begins to reopen May 2020.

Chuck went on to a long career in education, earning a doctorate in education from the University of Southern California, teaching, and serving as a school principal. He is currently an assistant superintendent responsible for Human Resources in a large Orange County school district. However, his love of surfing still beats powerfully in his heart. He frequently takes his entire family on international surfing trips. Photo below is a family surf trip to Nicaragua. Growing Up Venice has stayed with him.

Chuck and son Hank (left) surfing in Nicaragua. Photo courtesy of Chuck.

Chuck Lewis, a lifetime surfer, photo courtesy of Chuck

Chapter Eleven

Cultures Clash with Street Gangs

"Much has changed on the surface of Venice, but the heart and soul is still the same beautiful, dangerous place, it has always been." Diana Starr

The 1960's-1990's Brings Massive Cultural Changes

Clearly, growing up through the 40-50's, my sister, Jackie, and I were living between parallel cultural universes. We were side by side, yet worlds apart from the Beats down the street. While the Beats created their non-conforming stanzas, we completed our high school chemistry homework. Interestingly, other completely different kinds of parallel existences were simultaneously emerging, perhaps a mile away, in the Oakwood neighborhood and in the Ballona Wetlands.

While the Gas House patrons rallied at the beach, attracting Hippies as the 1960's rolled in, other cultural shifts were brewing nearby. A mere half mile away, poverty and social divides were escalating. Criminal street gangs began taking over the Oakwood area, or "Ghost Town" as it was known by the locals. The Shoreline Crips, a ferocious African-American gang, frequently warred against the Venice 13, a Mexican-American gang. Both were based in the Oakwood area of Venice. Gunfire became routine as rival gangs struggled over turf and the narcotics trade. Venice became known as one of the most dangerous, gang-filled, areas in all of Los Angeles, second only to Watts.

World Class Small Craft Harbor

Simultaneously, just across Washington Boulevard to the south, long-time oil derricks began to be replaced by earth movers. The federal government, in partnership with the County of Los Angeles, and in cooperation with the State of California, began construction on the largest man-made small-craft harbor in the United States. Marina del Rey was becoming a reality.

It is almost impossible to believe that as Hippies and Beats filled the nearby coffee houses, street gangs hijacked the streets at night, long-time residents locked their doors, while affluent young professionals dreamed of living in the high rise condos promised at the marina. All of this was going on within a few square miles at the same time. We will explore the coming of the marina in the next chapter.

Troubles in Oakwood

It may be that seeds for trouble were sown early in Venice's history. Back in 1905, when Abbot Kinney's romantic resort first opened, the hotels and restaurants needed support staff to cater to the affluent tourists. Certainly, the construction itself, dredging of the canals, and building the pier, required laborers. A great majority of those workers were African-American, and as such, were not permitted to live in white neighborhoods. They were relegated to a nearby area, away from the beach, called Oakwood. It was a mile square area west of Lincoln Boulevard between Washington and Venice Boulevards.

When Abbot Kinney died in 1920, he left his beautiful canal home at One Canal Street to his most trusted friend, chauffeur, and advisor, African-American, Irving Tabor. Early on, Kinney had observed the young janitor, Tabor, working hard on the Venice Pier. He admired him. One day he stopped Tabor and asked if he'd like to work for him. Of course, young Irving, immediately said yes. Kinney had just purchased a Model T car and it would soon be delivered. "You know how to drive young man?"

Kinney-Tabor home moved to Oakwood from 1 Canal Street to 1310 6th Avenue. Interestingly, this house is located one block east of Donna's grandfather's pharmacy on W. Washington Boulevard.

"Oh yes sir."

"Would you like to drive for me?"

"Oh yes sir!" agreed Tabor. Of course, he had never driven a car! The next day Tabor went to Santa Monica and found a man to teach him how to drive!

According to his daughter, Thelma Tabor Brawley in a 1990 *Los Angeles Times* interview, the two men became close, their friendship lasting across Kinney's life. Kinney's many business dealings required his presence across the country. Thus, Tabor drove Kinney across the United States. Tabor's daughter, Thelma, stated, "If a hotel wouldn't allow my dad to stay, due to race, Kinney would not stay there either. If it wasn't good enough for Tabor, it wasn't good enough for Kinney." She marveled at his egalitarian view of the world.

However, Kinney's neighbors at the Venice canal did not share his democratic ideals. Even though Tabor was legally willed the canal house, he was not allowed to live there due to racial covenants in the white neighborhood against African Americans. The neighbors made him feel so unwelcome, that he literally picked up his house, dividing it into two huge pieces, and floated them down the canal to Oakwood. Some historical reports say that he separated the house into three sections and trucked them away. Perhaps he floated sections on the canals, and then trucked them to Oakwood.

How Tabor accomplished the move is of little importance when compared to his contribution to the now historic Oakwood neighborhood. His association with Kinney brought gravitas to it, as did his building project. Tabor built a unique collection of lovely California-style-bungalows for the many family members whom he encouraged to migrate west from Louisiana where they easily found work in Venice-of-America. According to an August 2016 article in the *Los Angeles Times*, those Tabor bungalows sold for $5.8 million dollars!

Across the decades, Oakwood settled into a comfortable black neighborhood complete with a church and a sense of culture. Homeowners stayed for generations. It was home.

Oakwood Declines

As the years passed, Oakwood changed. What had been a vibrant, working class African-American suburb into the 1920's began to decline when the Great Depression hit in 1929. Joblessness, poverty, and hopelessness began to infect the neighborhood. As the pollutants from the nearby oil fields filtered through the area, choking the air and the canals, despair settled in. Without jobs, it was hard for people

Tabor physically moved Kinney's home to Oakwood. Photo June, 2020.

to maintain their homes and property.

The Oakwood area fell into disrepair. It became less family friendly. Law abiding residents began to drift away. Property values and rents plummeted. Low rents began to attract a criminal element. Drug traffickers found a foothold. The stage was set for the gang warfare that would strangle the Oakwood neighborhood for the next 50 years.

Criminal Activity

Venice became notorious for gang violence. I graduated from Santa Monica City College in 1962 and transferred to USC. I was home for weekends, however, my time was spent on the volleyball court in front of our house at 2909 Ocean Front and thinking about Ken. He was a frequent visitor. When we were not playing volleyball, we were strolling through Pacific Ocean Park, or having a soda along the boardwalk. By and large I kept to the beach. My father had a whole new family and I loved playing with all my little siblings. We laughed in the surf, and played tag on the beach. I was fairly oblivious to the shootings taking place a mile away, though, of course we had *always* been careful, especially at night.

When Jackie and I were old enough to drive, our father beseeched us with a valuable admonition. "If you are followed home, drive yourself into the Police Station on Venice Boulevard." That advice became extremely useful. On many occasions when I was driving home from school or work, especially in the dark, and a strange car would begin to tail me, I would simply drive to the Police Station. It always worked. The potential problem invariably drove past.

In the mid 1960's, my mother purchased a duplex on Venice Way, a block from the traffic circle. One night, she came home in the dark, and opened her front yard gate. Out of the corner of her eye, she glimpsed a big man in a brown leather jacket walking down the sidewalk toward her. She knew that if he were up to no good, she would be more vulnerable opening her front door. She stayed inside her three foot high picket gate. In an instant, he was upon her. He quickly reached across the fence and grabbed at her oversized bag. She resisted. He knocked her hard in the head. She was stunned for a moment, but did not fall down. He got the bag, ran off with it, and all her valuables.

She was terribly shaken up as she called the police. They arrived. She called her friend who lived nearby, to come and console her. His car would not start because someone had stolen its battery! It was a bad night. About a week later, the police returned her empty bag. They had found it in an alley. Shortly thereafter, she sold the property and moved to Westchester.

I understood that Venice could be dangerous. Certainly, there was never a time growing up that we did not use extreme caution, coming and going, keeping ourselves safe, locking the doors.

In 1964, Ken and I married and moved to Orange County. The larger picture of the dramatic cultural shifts taking place in Venice did not register on my radar. As the years passed, the nitty-gritty of living in Venice, the violence, and changes in demographics, seemed far away to me. Before long, my life became filled with babies and teaching school.

Demographic Changes

As the 1990's approached, locals demanded a stop to the gang violence. The result was that the police implemented a severe, zero tolerance regime. They cracked down, stopping anyone who looked suspicious. African-Americans claims of racism on the part of the police began to rise up. Long-time African-American residents cried out for justice. The gangs began to move out. However, claims of racial profiling, and accusations of planted evidence by the police left residents angry. They asserted that the police hassled African-American youths just for being black. Young black men in the neighborhood felt that they were being profiled. Racism has continued to be a problem in Venice with long established residents claiming harassment.

A 2020 Google search of street gangs on the Westside of Los Angeles, brings up a map with shaded areas showing where street gangs are active. In looking at the Westside gangs, the map shows that the Oakwood neighborhood into Culver City is held by the Venice 13. It is a Mexican-American gang, dating back to the late 1950's, long known as one of the most dangerous street gangs on the Westside. Its enemies include the African-American Shoreline Crips. The Venice 13 is reputed to have ties to the Mexican Mafia.

The map further shows gang activity in Santa Monica. The area is held by the Mexican-American gang, Santa Monica 13, founded in the 1920's. The enemies of this gang include: "Sotel, Venice 13,

First Baptist Church of Venice in 1911 before the church was on

1911 First Baptist Church Congregation – Save Venice Photo.

Culver City Boys, and the Graveyard Gangster Crips."

Against this backdrop of gang troubles, high tech businesses have found their way to Venice. Their employees, in addition to Hollywood film employees needing housing, have looked to old neighborhoods such as Oakwood. This influx of professionals is forcing gentrification on old, previously, dumpy areas of Venice. As this plethora of deep-pocket buyers has become available, prices have soared. Long established residents have seen an opportunity to cash in, a different kind of oil boom! Many have taken advantage of the opportunity and moved away.

Recently, Ken and I ventured northward once again, to take another look at Venice. This time we focused on the Oakwood neighborhood. I knew that buyers were purchasing homes as fast as they came on the market for big multi-million-dollar price tags.

We were frankly surprised, after all the stories we had heard about gangs and roughnecks, how beautiful and peaceful the neighborhood was. Our drive-by reconnaissance showed a lovely old neighborhood. It is filled with trees. There are many homes built during the Venice-of-America era. They are big, beautiful wooden Victorians. Some have bars on the windows, while others hide behind tall security fences. We saw no graffiti, nor signs of gang activity. In fact, we did not see anyone outside, in the middle of a warm June day. Clearly gentrification is taking place. The neighborhood has come to be seen as an important legacy of the role which African-Americans played in the building of Los Angeles. In 2008, the Kinney-Tabor home at 1320 Sixth Avenue in Oakwood, was designated as a Los

First Baptist Church 1960's building - subject of controversy. Photo June 2020

Angeles Historic Monument.

In addition, in 2017, the Los Angeles City Council approved historic preservation protections for the compound of bungalows which Irving Tabor built for his family in Oakwood during the 1920's. The *Los Angeles Times* article from 2016 noted earlier, referenced the property: *Venice compound with historic past hits the market for $5.8 million. The Argonaut* followed up with the story that Lisa Henson, daughter of "Muppets" creator, Jim Henson closed escrow on the compound for $5.4 million. The City's actions halted planned renovation of the bungalows. Any and all changes must now go through the Cultural Heritage Commission for adherence to federal historic rehabilitation guidelines. It was a grassroots effort on the part of concerned Venice residents which called the City's attention to the

Black Lives Matter memorial on church steps. Photo June 2020

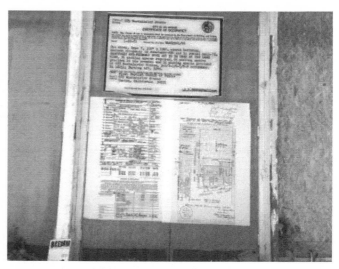

Plans for church building - a private home. Photo June 2020

historic nature of the compound.

The legacy of the African-American contribution to the building of Los Angeles is exemplified in Oakwood. There is concern in Venice that the African-American population in the Oakwood area has been in decline since 1980, (9.6% in the 80's to 5.6% today). The new demographic changes have been met with horror by some long-time Venetians. There are many who obsess over the idea that if developers have their way, the bohemian Venice they love, with its broad range of people will disappear. James R. Smith in his *Gentrifying Paradise* (2019) says: "What I have enjoyed most about Venice has been the people. Venetians come in all colors, ages, and educational levels…most were well informed about politics and bigger issues such as life and death and a meaningful life."

At this writing, another conflict regarding gentrification is brewing in Oakwood. *LA Times* headline: *Should a former Black church in Venice be turned into a mansion for a white family?* (July 5, 2020). The First Baptist Church of Venice sat empty for years, its congregation moved to another locale. It was sold to multi-millionaire couple Jay Penske and his wife, publishers of *Rolling Stone* and *Variety* magazines. Penske spent $6.3 million on the church and its parking lot, plus another $5.5 million on a second parking lot across the street. They want to build a huge house. The Penskes thought they would be welcome. Church members say they paid fair price. The church did not meet requirements for historic site designation. The ill feelings and conflicts continue as many believe their neighborhood is being sold out and could lose its significance in Black history.

Guest Article by Diana Starr

For a moment let's step back to the 70's and 80's and glimpse what life was like, Growing Up Venice for my youngest sister, Diana. She is a full generation behind me. Diana has generously written a response to my questions about what her life was like.

My Venice Childhood
by Diana Ray (Lewis) Starr

Growing up in Venice Beach, California was sometimes glorious, and other times terrifying. I was born in 1970 and spent the entirety of my childhood within approximately a mile of Venice Beach, moving between three homes that my parents owned. My first home was at 2909 Ocean Front Walk, a three-story gray and stucco monstrosity of a building. My dad built it with the help of his older girls and my mother. I am the youngest of eight children and the house could certainly accommodate all of us. By the time I was a preteen, Dad had converted the top deck of the building to a huge

carpeted indoor playroom with swings. We had a blast playing up there, looking out over the ocean.

My parents divorced and our mother bought a nice three-bedroom home on a double lot with a huge back yard less than a mile away, 641 Oxford Avenue. She paid $40,000 for that home with a detached garage. This house is situated on a diagonal tract with an alley splitting it down the middle. The house was literally on the other side of the tracks; the railroad ran along a stretch of property directly across the street from that home. It came through once per evening. I have a very early memory of running outside with my brothers to place pennies on the track. After the train rumbled by, we would collect our flattened copper prizes.

My first truly terrifying life experience happened while in that neighborhood. My best friend lived at the end of the block and every day we would play together after school. It was 1977 and I was in the 2nd grade. I bounced my Hippity Hop down the block to Lori's house and proceeded to bounce out front while she finished up her chores.

A man drove up in a yellow sedan and called out a hello. He said something I couldn't hear, and then pulled into the alley. He said hello again and said he needed help with directions. I hopped over to him just as he started to open the car door. Before I knew what happened, he had me wrapped in his arms and was pulling me toward the driver's seat. Adrenaline must have kicked in. I pulled and fought hard and managed to get free. I started to run home and heard his car peel off a screech as he made his getaway. My friend, Lori's big brother, Scottie, heard the ruckus and looked out the bedroom window, but didn't get a good look at the attacker. The police were called. I was very lucky to get away like I did!

My sister, Cindy, who is two years my senior, still occupies the Oxford home. Instead of a railroad across the street, today there are $5M houses. The Venice we grew up in has had a major facelift in the past thirty years.

The third home I lived in was a small beach cottage located only six buildings away from my father's. That house was at 2815 Ocean Front Walk. It stands out as the most remarkable of locations during my young life. It was here that I became a conscious human being and learned the most about the world.

The building itself was quite unremarkable. It embodied the classic Venice bohemian vibe. It was a chance for my mother to save money and rent out the Oxford house. I was happy with the idea of living on the beach again, if not a little heartbroken to leave my elementary school and best friend down the block.

Life on the beach for a latchkey kid was certainly interesting. While my mother worked all the time, I spent many unsupervised hours playing in the waves, building sand sculptures and meeting strangers, tourists mostly. I remember making a new friend one day, a young teen-age boy from Japan. I showed him how to use the seaweed as a shawl and become a sea princess. I showed him where the sand crabs dug down as the waves pulled out. We were pen pals for years after.

One notable year was 1983 when a massive storm took out the concrete entrance under the new Venice Pier at the foot of Washington Boulevard. The waves were so large and strong that they rolled under the deck of the bungalow and flooded the Speedway! I'll never forget all the neighbors out that night, madly filling sandbags to prevent the water from filling their homes and apartments. Luckily, our little bungalow was a good 4 feet off the ground. The day after the storm was filled with hunting for treasure and I even scored a new boogie board. The power of that storm was a testament to why we had so many piers fall in the past.

The cottage was little more than a two-room bungalow, but it was classic "old Venice." After we moved out, back to Oxford, a film company rented it. They filmed the cult classic *Summer School*, starring Mark Harmon.

At a young age, maybe eight or nine, I learned to be streetwise. The building next door to our cottage held a fascinating collection of people. We called the place the "Heartbreak Hotel." There was an ever-changing rotation of renters. I'm pretty sure some of the apartments weren't used for just living. These were party people and I suspect it was frequently used as a brothel. I only entered that building one time, when a boy my age moved in with his mother and invited me into his apartment. I was not surprised that I had my first kiss in that place.

Summers were wild on the beach. It seemed like millions of people would walk the path between the Venice Pier and the Windward Avenue circus of Muscle Beach. The bored "Heartbreak Hotel" tenants would tie dollar bills to fishing lines and prank on the tourists who would reach for the bills as it was dragged away, as if by the sea breeze. One summer those same tenants glued coins to the concrete and had their laughs watching the tourists try to pick them up.

The big spectacle was 4th of July. The music blared, the drinking was heavy, and then as night fell, the beach turned into a virtual battleground. Bunkers were dug and

bottle rockets placed to attack. My brothers took m80s (short pieces of dynamite) and threw them into the surf, lighting up the incoming waves. This was before Los Angeles banned the use of fireworks and it was common for everyone to hit Tijuana, Mexico to get the good ones for the occasion.

My hobby, during my early teens, was to roller skate as fast as I could down the bike path. I have the scars to prove it. Skating was "the thing" at the time, per Olivia Newton-John's fantasy film *Xanadu*, based in Venice. I could race down the bike path and practice tricks during the week, but never on the busy weekends.

Muscle Beach at Windward Avenue was a good twenty-minute walk for me, and I never went alone. There were too many bums and druggies and people that would want to take advantage of a little girl alone. We had plenty of perverts down the Speedway trying to show us their privates as it was. On the opposite side of my universe was the Marina del Rey peninsula, a high-end planned section of real estate with A-Z alphabet streets. Actor Dudley Moore could often be seen there, driving in his Rolls Royce.

Anchorage Elementary [the site of the former Nightingale Elementary School] was a wonderful little school located just on the other side of Washington Boulevard. I'll never forget how safe it felt at that school. They provided our lunches and we just needed to remember to bring a dime for a cold milk. I recall teaching my classmates the "hukilau" dance I had learned in Hawaii during winter break. It was also where I made a lifelong friend, Zoe.

Zoe and I became instant sisters and spent all the time we could together. Zoe lived with a single mom on Linnie Canal and her front yard was almost as exciting a playground as mine. The one-bedroom duplex sat on the canal, with a large patio and a huge weeping willow tree. It was shady and safe, and we played with our dolls and plastic horses, and read our Nancy Drew novels there. We would

Diana with Zoe, holding her cat Journey

venture down to the main road sometimes to play in the tiny playground. We never felt unsafe there, but we did need to check the homeless situation out first. It was common to find an old drunk or mentally ill person sleeping in the little "hut" built for children.

Zoe was an only child and her mom worked all day at a sail maker's shop. Zoe taught me many things during our time on the canals, including how to make some really great tuna sandwiches. I learned domestic skills from her and her mother, Pepper. They took me on as another child as much as I took them on as my new family.

Safe and serene Linnie Canal

The canals were *the* artsy bohemian place to live in Venice in the early 80's, if you were lucky enough to find a vacancy. The canals themselves were filthy, filled with refuse and duck dung. We rarely got into the water for fear of cutting our feet on broken glass or picking up a bird disease. However, the canals were safe to venture on by rowboat or barge. During the holiday season, a local group of residents pulled out a large barge, placed a piano on it and loaded everyone up to travel the canals and sing Christmas carols. That was one of my most magical childhood memories. My friends, Pepper and Zoe always included me on fun occasions.

Zoe and I attended Mark Twain Junior High School together and graduated in 1985. It was a tough school, but we had a great group of friends that made it bearable. It didn't help that my parents drove around in Corvettes and most of the families that lived in that part of Venice could barely scrape together the rent. I was called "rich bitch" and bullied often, but my friends had my back. While all my friends continued on to Venice High School, I had the opportunity to attend my elder siblings' alma mater, Santa Monica High. It was destiny, as I met my husband, Richard Starr, on my first day of high school in 1985. We are still married and have two beautiful boys.

Linnie Canal Play park, c. 1980

Richard and I left California after the 1992 riots and stayed away for about 15 years. I now live 20 miles away in San Pedro. Rich commutes to Playa Vista where he works as a creative director for Electronic Arts.

We still enjoy visiting Venice a few times a year. Much has changed on the surface, but the heart and soul is still the same beautiful, dangerous place it has always been. I like to take my kids to the boardwalk in all its lewd glory. When friends come from out of state to visit, I will take them on the grand LA tour and sometimes even take them skating. Once a Venice girl, always a Venice girl!

Diana and friend skating c. 2001

America Reacts in Social Unrest May-July 2020

I have enjoyed sharing some pieces of "lost" Los Angeles history with you during these long months of pandemic lockdown. However, at week eleven, over Memorial weekend on Monday May 25th, 2020, a case of police brutality set off a firestorm of protests. During this pandemic, America has suffered 30% unemployment. All businesses not considered "essential" have been closed down. The economic catastrophe to citizens has been devastating, combined with the emotional toll of being mandated to stay inside for weeks on end. It has created a tinderbox. Tragically, the match which lit it was the death of an unarmed man in police custody. Social unrest has rocked the United States for a month at this writing.

During the felony arrest of African-American, George Floyd, four Minneapolis police officers restrained him. One officer, Derek Chauvin, restricted him by pressing his knee to Floyd's neck. With his face pressed to the cement, Floyd croaked out, "*I can't breathe!*" Chauvin kept his knee on Floyd's neck for 8:47 seconds while the other three officers looked on. Floyd died. The incident was videotaped and widely shown through news outlets. The brutality of the incident, coupled with other similar cases of African-Americans dying while in police custody, has provoked protests and civil unrest across the country for the past few weeks. To add to the agony, lootings and murders have hijacked some of the peaceful protests.

America is in an uproar at I write this. The Minneapolis City Council has disbanded its police force, stating that it is "rotten down to its infrastructure." Minneapolis authorities are working on police reform. Politicians and law enforcement departments in major metropolitan areas are reviewing their arrest protocols. The officers involved in the Floyd death have been arrested. Chauvin has been charged with second degree murder, while the other three have been charged with aiding and abetting murder in the second degree. Protests across America, in the name of "Black Lives Matter," call for change and justice. As young Americans march in the streets of America, chanting, *I can't breathe*, similar demonstrations continue to take place across the globe. Hundreds of thousands of protesters have taken to the streets in Kenya, Great Britain, France, and Germany. The world is calling for an end to discrimination based upon color.

The New York Times reported in a July 3, 2020 article that this Black Lives Matter movement may be the biggest movement in United States history. It reported that on June 6, at the peak of protests, that day alone, half a million people turned out in 550 places across the U.S. "What's more, the reignited movement has created actionable change since citizens began taking to the streets following Floyd's killing." The article continued, "recent polls suggest that about 15-26 million people in the United States have participated in demonstrations over the death of George Floyd and others in recent weeks."

Looking back at the story of early Venice, when Mr. Tabor inherited Abbot Kinney's home, we see that discrimination has been present since the beginning of our Venice story. Of course, it goes back some 400 years to the founding of our country. At this writing, perhaps more Americans in positions of power are taking the demonstrations for racial equality seriously. As this story goes to press, the social unrest is far from over.

This mural was painted on the side of highway in Milan, Italy and the photo of it was widely circulated on the Internet in May 2020.

Venice and Change

Change continues to affect the cultures of the area. About ten years ago, the social influencing Tech Industry discovered the unique advantages of operating in Venice, Santa Monica, and Playa Vista. Tech companies admired the area's proximity to the Los Angeles International Airport, reasonable rent, the area's great weather, its youthful Bohemian vibe, and its close proximity to Hollywood.

The area has evolved into a business hub for the electronics industry. As of 2019, it was estimated that 140,000 new jobs have opened up in the area, including 500 start-ups and electronics firms setting up shop. This beach area has become known as "Silicon Beach." Neighborhoods like Oakwood are becoming gentrified so quickly, that home buyers in the area are sometimes oblivious to the fact that the neighborhood has had its share of problems. Venice is undergoing yet another massive change in industry and population, another "universe" has cast its spell over the area.

As California has slowly begun to open up, beaches, parks, and some businesses, Ken and I decided to venture out to take another look at Venice. This time we visited the buildings occupied by Google on Main Street in Venice. I wanted to see the famous Binoculars building designed by architect Frank Gehry. I'll tell more about that in the next chapter.

Ken and I drove by my grandfather's old storefront on Abbot Kinney Boulevard. The windows on many of the businesses were boarded up, as demonstrations and riots had been going on in the area. The Black Lives Matter protest in nearby Santa Monica a few weeks before was taken over by looters. They broke the windows of the Nordstrom store in the Santa Monica Promenade Mall and made off with inventory.

My husband and I have lived through three-quarters of a century of cultural change in America. Much has been violent and brutal, but much has also been peaceful, creative, and beautiful. We have learned that change is inevitable, a constant. It is essential that it be carefully managed which is society's difficult challenge.

Lake Ballona c. 1903. After Wicks stopped construction on his Port Ballona the area went back to its natural state. USC Library, Pierce Photography Collection

Chapter Twelve

Another Universe: A World Class Harbor in the Ballona Wetlands

"We are tied to the ocean. And when we go back to the sea, whether it is to sail or to watch-we are going back from whence we came." John F. Kennedy

Astonishingly, while the Oakwood neighborhood was undergoing dramatic changes, so was the acreage adjacent to Washington Boulevard on the other side of the street. The Ballona Wetlands were being dredged for a world-class small craft harbor. Yet another parallel world was evolving.

The first thoughts about constructing a harbor in the wetlands began clear back in 1887. That's right. It is not a typo. In 1887, under the auspices of the Santa Fe Railroad, a visionary named M.C. Wicks formed the Port Ballona Development Company. His idea was to turn the estuary into a major commercial port to serve Los Angeles. He went so far as to raise $300,000 and supervised its construction for three years. Unfortunately, an economic depression in 1893 set off a panic resulting in financial havoc in the United States. Railroads had overbuilt and their shaky financing forced banks into failure. It was a terrible series of financial disasters and Mr. Wicks was forced into bankruptcy. The Port Ballona Development Company failed. Slowly, the would-be harbor returned to a duck hunter's haven.

Twenty-five years later, the idea again got traction. However, the Army Corps of Engineers, after an intensive study, voted no, bad idea. In 1937 Congress was back to thinking about a harbor for Los Angeles. The County Board of Supervisors called for a study. There was a competition. San Pedro won out. The Port of Los Angeles was built and is managed by the Los Angeles Harbor Department. It occupies 7500 acres of land and water, adjoined to the separate Port of Long Beach.

The idea of some kind of harbor closer to Los Angeles kept returning. By the 1950's the plan for a port had grown into an ambitious inspiration to create the nation's largest man-made marina. Its name was to be The Playa del Rey Inlet and Harbor of Venice, California. Proponents felt that it would be difficult to sell a project with such a complicated name. It was soon shortened to the more manageable "Marina del Rey."

In 1954 President Eisenhower signed Public Law 780, allowing the concept of a Federal harbor project. The deal was that Los Angeles County had to pay 50% toward the building of it. Bonds were offered and the voters of Los Angeles voted yes. Thus the harbor became reality.

By November of 1958, the channel jetties had been built, creating the entrance to the harbor. Shortly afterward a few facilities were constructed. Unfortunately, in the winter of 1962-63 a storm tore through the young harbor resulting in considerable damage. The marina was vulnerable to wave action. In an emergency move, the County implemented a temporary solution. Protection was provided by constructing protective sheet-pile baffles at the entrance to the channel. Soon the U.S. Corps of Engineers came up with a permanent solution against damaging waves. That solution was to build a breakwater at the entrance to the harbor.

In the spring of 1962, I attended my first-ever event in the new marina. The Sheraton Hotel had officially opened its doors. As members of the Santa Monica College student government, we rented its ballroom and hosted our end-of- the-year festivities. I recall that the hotel sat on one of the short

Construction of a World Class Marina del Rey from Marshland c. 1960. Photo courtesy Argonaut News.

peninsulas known as "keys". It was barren. The boat docks had not yet been built. There were no plantings, no trees nor grass. As I scanned the area, heavy earth-moving tractors were hard at work. We students could intellectualize that a marina was coming, we could see the water and the construction, but the vision of high-rise buildings, traffic, Trader Joe's, a Cheesecake Factory, or any of all that was coming, was beyond our imaginations.

I remember pausing a moment that night as I left the banquet. It was getting dark and the giant earth movers were silent. In the quiet, I could hear the soft lapping of the waves against the bulk head. I thought back to my childhood. As I looked across the stretch of water, I tried to visualize where the old dump had once been. I looked west and thought about Hoppyland. It was lost to time by then, but the fun of it was still in my memory. I was nostalgic that night; for the wide open spaces that had once been. I knew that the improvements would provide lovely amenities, that the harbor would be a beautiful addition to Venice, and to Los Angeles, but still, it was so changed...

Beautiful high-rise condominium Marina del Rey. photo 2020.

Marina del Rey Opens

By 1965, Marina del Rey, after twelve years of construction, and the successful solution of its big wave problems, officially opened. Its total cost was $36 million dollars. Today it is thriving, a huge asset to Los Angeles. One of its claims to fame is that it is the largest man-made small craft harbor in North America with 5000 boat slips.

In the 70-80's the marina was considered the "in" spot for swinging singles. In fact the *Los Angeles Times* described the area as "a notoriously active outpost for LA's 'swinging single scene.'" The *Times* further reported that Dennis Wilson of the Beach Boys fame dove so enthusiastically into the marina scene that he never came back up. In fact, in some quarters, California's soft rock music became known as "yacht rock" inspired by the Marina del Rey set.

Nearly fifty years later, well into the 21st century, Marina del Rey has once again hit its stride and is trending as a cool place to be. In addition, it is a good value for tech workers looking for housing. A 2016 news story reported that the average price per square foot to live in Venice was around $1000 per square foot for a single-family home. The marina's high rise could offer housing at the more affordable prices. Marina del Rey is yet another parallel universe. This "universe" is peopled by upscale, affluent youthful professionals. The 8,600 residents enjoy a comfortable lifestyle in luxury high rise buildings. There are fine dining opportunities in its restaurants. Plus there's shopping in trendy boutiques. The harbor includes miles of biking and jogging trails. On weekends, families visit the Fisherman's Village at the water's edge. The marina enjoys a culture unto its own, which is very different from some of the troubles that have taken place a mere few blocks away.

Beautiful yachts fill the world class small craft harbor

Fisherman's Village Marina del Rey

Large custom single family homes line the streets and canal on the western
section of Marina del Rey Photo June 2020

Lovely custom homes - Marina del Rey. Photo June 2020

Chapter Thirteen

Cultures Collide Yet Again - Gentrification

"The only constant in life is change"- Heraclitus.

The Rise of Silicon Beach

Profoundly, computer pioneer Steve Jobs, once proclaimed, "Of all the inventions of humans, the computer is the most awesome tool ever invented." Clearly it has changed humanity from the Industrial Age to the Information Age. Such changes have rippling effects. Venice is being bowled over by one of its ripples.

Venice now rivals the Bay Area's Silicon Valley as the country's premier tech hub!

It is almost unbelievable that Venice could evolve into so many chameleon-like iterations. It is a marvel that it can contain so many universes within its small boundaries. We have seen its magical Venice-of-America version; its productivity as the state's fourth most important oil field; its amusement value to hundreds of thousands of Angelenos who have flocked to its piers; and its mania as a surfing and outdoor roller skating capital. We have witnessed the eccentricities of its writers and artists; its powerful *Main Street* for Jewish immigrants; its Hippie invasion; its decline during and after the Great Depression; its distress as dangerous gangs brought violence; its attractiveness as an industry filming locale; its tourist value as the number two "must see" destination in Los Angeles; its development of the country's largest man-made small boat harbor. And now we see its rise as a global center for the electronic technology industry.

This evolution as a technical center began about a decade ago. In 2011 Google opened a new campus in

Binoculars Building at Google's Venice Campus. Photo May 2020

Venice on Main Street. That campus stretches across three buildings, adjoined by the iconic post-modern Binoculars Building designed by architect Frank Gehry and artists Claes Oldenberg and Coosje van Bruggen.

Soon other tech giants began taking notice, thinking about the easy access to Los Angeles International Airport, reasonable rents, and the fun, eclectic vibe of Venice. Nine years later, other big deal electronics technology firms are well established neighbors. The shift has been so phenomenal that the area has been dubbed "Silicon Beach." News stories claim that it rivals the San Francisco Bay Area's Silicon Valley as a technology capital. (*Discover Los Angeles*, Mar 14, 2019)

The area defined as Silicon Beach is the real estate stretching between southern Santa Monica, through Venice, bordered on the south by Playa Vista. You recall that Playa Vista is the high-rise neighborhood which grew up out of the Wetlands previously occupied by Hughes Aircraft. Today Playa Vista is home to Yahoo, Microsoft, and Facebook, and thousands of jobs.

One of the most significant cultural changes to affect Venice, perhaps since cars were invented, was the arrival of these tech companies. The new arrivals included something like 500 start-ups and

Many Venetians decry gentrification

electronics firms. My brother-in-law, Rich Starr, works as a video game development director at Electronic Arts in Playa Vista. His title is "Creative Director." His company is the second largest gaming company in the Americas and Europe. It has been a pioneer in the home gaming industry. They develop and distribute video games for game consoles, personal computers, mobile phones and the Internet. Some of their products are the "Battlefield" series which Rich worked on six years ago. Other games include, "Command and Conquer," "Star Wars: Jedi Fallen Order," and more. They also produce sports titles such as: "FIFA Soccer", "Madden NFL," "NBA Live," NHL", and EA Sports UFC."

The street on which the company's Los Angeles area campus is located is "EA Way," for Electronic Arts. Its state-of-the-art game studio in Playa Vista, includes 250,000 square feet and can accommodate expansion.

A review of the company's website illustrates the attractiveness of Southern California for the technical industry. The EA Los Angeles website states: *Working in Los Angeles means year-round sunny weather, access to a myriad of outdoor activities and proximity to a world-renown entertainment industry.*

It seems fitting as we close our story of Venice in its many facets, that we come to discover that now, in the 21st Century, the most creative, new industry on the planet, finds itself drawn to the eccentricity, the brilliance, the outrageousness, and the creative culture of Venice as a setting to inspire creativity in its employees.

However, many aspects which have attracted this new industry to the area, may ironically become Venice's downfall. The tech industry translates into massive population shifts as families move to the "Silicon Beach" area, putting pressure on real estate values. Books such as *Gentrifying Paradise* by resident James R. Smith (2019), mentioned earlier, decry the invasion of white collar elites taking up residence in Venice. His writing traces the resistance movement against Venice becoming another Santa Monica "Third Street Promenade." Smith makes a case against big corporate chain stores. He believes that big chains, sniffing out profits, ruin an area. So far Venetians have resisted big national stores. He cites SoHo Manhattan as a *sad* example. He notes that what was once eccentric is now described in the official NYCgo.com website as: "This trendy neighborhood is one of Manhattan's fashion capitals— SoHo, the famously arty neighborhood of the 70's and 80's has evolved into one of the New York City's prime shopping districts." That is the opposite of what some long-time residents want for the future of Venice. They want to preserve as much of its individuality as possible.

However, preservation has a big downside. An article in the *Atlantic Magazine* entitled, "How Venice Beach Became a Neighborhood for the Wealthy," (July 24, 2017), says it well. The story explores the anti-growth fervor of existing homeowners in older communities, such as Venice, who resist development of adequate housing for all who would desire to live there. The point is that because growth has been deliberately stunted in Venice across the last few decades, property values are driven up. The conclusion: "thus guaranteeing that this geographically, small, highly desirable enclave by the ocean will lose its bohemian vibe, ending up as a neighborhood for the increasingly old and very rich, like Laguna Beach, La Jolla, and Carmel-by-the Sea."

SOLD MAR 18, 2019

2308 Grand Canal   Off M
Venice, CA 90291

$4,888,952   **4**   **5**   **3,265**
Redfin Estimate   Beds   Baths   Sq. Ft.

Redfin Realty Ad from 2019 - Sold

In another story in the *Los Angeles Times,* writer, Robin Abcabian, makes this argument: *"They Discover, they gentrify, they ruin: How "progress" is wrecking Los Angeles Neighborhoods."* Her 2017 piece describes what has happened to Venice now that it has been discovered. She writes about her trials trying to find a parking place on Abbot Kinney Boulevard where she tried to meet up for a coffee. She stated: "Unfortunately in 2012 *GQ Magazine* named [Abbot Kinney] "the coolest block in America.""

This controversy over land use development is an old one. The unconventional vibe is celebrated as something to be preserved. Its attractiveness is the very quality of its demise. I appreciate that the scene at the end of Windward Avenue on the boardwalk is like no other in the world. Nowadays, I have small stake in Venice, in that it holds a special place in my heart. For four generations my family has lived and played there.

Venice may be heading toward an enclave for the old and rich, but there are still very serious social issues which need to be addressed. Los Angeles has something over 50,000 homeless, many of whom have migrated to Venice and Santa Monica.

I did a quick Zillow "houses-for-sale" search regarding housing prices in Venice. I found a recent sale. It was a 3100 square foot house on the Grand Canal which had listed at $4.5 million, and sold for

Gentrification: condominium buildings line the beach. This is 4411 Ocean Front. I took the photo in May 2020 to remind me that the edge of the building is where our front gate was in 1945. I spent much of my childhood at this spot.

over $5 million. Clearly much of the real estate has sky-high price tags. Smith's book details the very low rents of tenants in some of the old hotels which were converted to tiny apartments, decades ago. They provide low-income housing with ocean views. Many of the tenants are Section 8, low-income renters.

I don't have any answers. The influx of professional families purchasing property in the Oakwood area is probably deemed a positive change for some, as the majority of gang members have been forced out. That influx of people cannot help but push low-income dwellers with ocean views out. I am certain that many of the low-income dwellers are part of what creates the funky, crazy scene that attracts tourists. It may be impossible to have it all; a funky, gritty vibe and homes for high income residents. It probably is impossible. The economics of maintaining the diversity of a place like Venice are complicated.

Santa Monica's Ocean Park area by the pier had a freaky, exciting vibe across my childhood. However as time passed, it was deemed a dilapidated eyesore by the Santa Monica City Council. In 1959 Santa Monica established a Redevelopment Agency to take on the *upgrade* along the waterfront from Nielson Way to the Venice boundary, and east to Ocean Park Boulevard. Its purpose was to deal with the "blight" of the Ocean Park Pier and the surrounding area.

The Ocean Park Pier, POP, area declined c. 1970.

Today, two seventeen story condominium giants, with 250 rental apartments in each, stand there set in a public park. It looks nice, in a sanitized sort of way. There is no evidence that the historic Ocean Park Pier ever existed, nor is there a trace of the colorful little mom and pop shops that lined the boardwalk. I know it's probably progress, but oh how I loved the piers and all the excitement.

Changes in American Cities

Later, as I contemplated Ocean Park and all that it no longer was, I shared my thoughts with Ken. We were sitting at the end of the day, chatting over a cold drink, a habit we had perfected during the lockdown.

Sitting back in his chair, Ken began, "Donna you understand that what you are witnessing, what you are reading about, is demographic change. As real estate in downtown areas becomes too expensive, workers who live there are pushed out into the periphery, to the suburbs. We have seen it all over America. As the population shifts outwardly, soon businesses, schools, and industry follow. Suddenly there are workers for industry in the outskirts. After a generation or so, the downtown areas begin to empty out, decline, and low-income residents can afford to move back in."

He paused. "When we were in college in the 60's, don't you remember that downtown LA was something of a ghost town? When we married in 1964, we had our choice of brand new housing in outlying areas like Huntington Beach. As freeways were built to accommodate cars, the suburbs thrived, and the inner city of Los Angeles declined."

He learned forward and looked me in the eye. "Remember how shocked we were a few years ago when you had that book awards dinner at LA Live? We couldn't believe the foot traffic. The bright lights. We felt like we had suddenly fallen into Times Square! It was not the LA we had known."

"Ken, I think you are right." I added. "In general, we humans do not embrace change all that well. I guess I am sad to see so much of what I loved, obliterated."

Ken continued. "Venice is experiencing the same thing. It contracted during the Depression. After World War II, the soldiers returned and moved into the instant new communities which sprouted up all

One of two high rises which replaced the old homes and mom and pop grocery stores along the Ocean Park Pier area of Santa Monica. Photo 2020.

over in outlying areas. Jobs followed. Schools and parks opened. Venice suffered from population decline. Old buildings on Windward which were not up to code, such as the famous St. Marks Hotel,

Beautiful Victorians from the era of Venice of America. Well taken care of in 2020.

were torn down. Cheap rents were available in the old hotels, now converted to apartments. Remember the fabulous Del Mar Club in Santa Monica? Resort to the Stars. "

I nodded. "Remember, it became Synanon, a refuge for drug addicts, a rehabilitation center. The entire area contracted."

Ken paused and took a breath. "With Marina del Rey, Silicon Beach, and freeway-close to Hollywood, others with bigger pocketbooks began moving in. Now the suburbs are too far out. But there are issues of inadequate parking and availability of affordable housing. What you are witnessing in a small way, is what has happened to cities all over America."

He smiled as he summed up his ideas. "You have been writing about change. Your goal was to describe a piece of *lost* Los Angeles history. Maybe you discovered more change than you intended."

I thought about what he said, about the day he and I strolled through the side streets by Brooks Avenue, leading to the boardwalk. I had taken pleasure in photographing some of the historic homes remaining from the days of Abbot Kinney. Most have fresh paint and look immaculate.

I understand why it is important for the resistance in Venice to keep up the pressure to preserve what is left. They lost the fight to keep the post office building as a public building. The little shops that once lined the

Homes from the 1911 era of Abbot Kinney's Venice-of-America. Photo 2020.

boardwalk in Ocean Park are just memories now of the lucky few who are still around to remember.

Change is here, but how it will be accomplished is still negotiable. There are many more battles yet to fight.

1930's Post Office sold to private party.

Windward Traffic Circle in front of the Post Office is the former Lagoon of Venice-of-America

Chapter Fourteen

A Last Look

"They say you can never go home again, but maybe you can." Donna Friess

As California began to slowly reopen after the pandemic lockdown, Ken and I decided to venture out once more for another look at Venice. We specifically set out to visit the buildings occupied by Google on Main Street in Venice, and to study the neighborhood of Oakwood.

I wanted to see the very important Binoculars building designed by architect Frank Gehry. He is famed for his unusual designs around the world and at Los Angeles' Walt Disney Concert Hall. When we arrived, Ken pulled into a loading zone. I hopped out. As I sprinted toward a good photo spot, I looked down the street to Rose Avenue. A fleeting moment from the past washed over me, as I thought of my 15-year-old self, jockeying for a parking place near the Smart and Final store that had been in the next block.

Binoculars Building - No one around. June 2020.

I snapped some photos. Google occupies all three of Gehry's structures which comprise the buildings united through the street art which is a pair of two-story high binoculars. I noted the high security at the buildings, the locked garages, and the fact that no one seemed to be inside. Californians, by and large, were still working from home, late into the month of June.

I did not take long. As I loped back to the car, I scanned the large homeless encampment in the vacant lot next door. As Ken started the engine, we remarked that the entire block in front of the Google buildings was packed with RV's, the rolling homes of many marginally homeless people.

Thoughts

As an historian, I look back across all we have seen and talked about, from the Indigenous People through to the present. I am proud that generations of my family, including myself, have lived over 120 years of Venice's back story. I can't help but laugh as I imagine my grandparents buying the lot at 4411 Ocean Front Walk, just twenty feet from a working oil well for $1000. Nor can I imagine what my parents were thinking when they made the decision to raise their family in an oil field. As my brother Chuck mentioned in his article, "It was a silly place to raise kids." Maybe it was silly, but all of us Lewis kids have had an experience unlike most others who grew up in more conventional neighborhoods. It was an oddly, unusual experience Growing Up Venice.

I cannot help but think about the role of "place" in terms of one's psychological development. Place Attachment Theory is about the relationship between a person and their emotional attachment to their experiences in a particular place. I understand that in many real ways I am a child of Venice. I do recall the immense feeling of peace which overcame me the day that I walked around the condominium building which occupies the site of my growing up, at 4411. That day, as I looked out across the sand, to the ocean, a great feeling of calm overtook me. I did not say anything to Ken, but in the weeks which have followed, sometimes as I am going to sleep, I feel that sense of calm. Perhaps it is merely the understanding that I started there, and that it has all worked out for me. I don't know, but I felt it. It was exquisite. They say, "you can never go home again," but maybe that day I did.

As the years passed, and I grew to adulthood, unbound by childhood, living in the larger world, I felt a certain urgency to be "normal." The experiences I had growing up, wandering free amidst wildly different people from myself, deeply influenced the *who* of my character. It worked to define the person I would become. Perhaps it influenced my studious habits, my commitment to financial security, my sense of responsibility, my tenacity. It was dangerous, beautiful and outrageous, all at the same time. It affected me in ways I probably cannot define. It is and was a place of vast complexity.

I know that witnessing people struggling with inadequate

Donna's old nei8ghborhood. "Place" for Donna all these years later still holds a magic. The houses she knew are gone now, but a warm flush of peace overcame over her as she stood where she had once lived. Photo May 2020. Today this is known as Marina Peninsula.

resources, living hand-to-mouth, and moment to moment, made a deep impression on me. I remember that my little friend in first grade, Julie Ann, didn't have a dime for her cocoa [I met up with Julie Ann in high school and we enjoyed a friendship.] I know that I had only one dress. Growing up like that illustrated for me, in a deep way, that I did not want to create a life that was not firmly anchored by security; financial and emotional.

I know that living on the edge of the continent awakened a primal part of me which is most at home in open spaces. Ken and I have celebrated our rural life, our long unlimited vistas, every day, for the last half century. It is also probable that Venice showed me a way to be sensitive toward people who do not look like me, allowed me a comfort level with others which has served me across my life. It was a different way to grow up, and I appreciate all that it taught me.

My take-aways from these months of studying and thinking about Venice are many. Foremost, I am captivated by the recent epiphany I had regarding the existence of so many parallel cultures. I see that they have existed always, and remain today. Until this project, I had never thought much about them. My mind has been blown by what I have learned. Venice is a microcosm of complexity, a cauldron of the unusual. Perhaps it is a reflection of our greater culture; its intricacies, its difficulties, and complications, which are envied around the world.

As I close down the computer and conclude this story, I cannot help but smile, thinking about those two little blonde girls, stooped over the oily waters in the Grand Canal, dipping their guppy-catching nets into the water. I see those girls roaming the beaches, collecting sea glass and bottle caps; enjoying endless sunny days in the gently rolling waves, just outside their

Jackie and Donna 1948 Venice Beach

175

front gate. They are tanned little girls who will grow up into strong professional women, but in their hearts will retain an understanding of the importance of celebrating all kinds of places and all kinds of people. They will grasp the complexities of the many parallel universes which signify the fabric of American life.

Donna and Jackie, Snow at the Beach. 1948. Looking for shells in the surf line.

Family Photo Gallery

Charles H. V. Lewis - Great grandfather - Venice Pier looking south, January 1908

Charles H.V. Lewis at Venice Pier c. 1910

Charles Lewis State Senator making an appearance c. 1920's Venice Beach Picnic. Great grandfather Charles back left.

Great grandmother pharmacist Lydia Cram Lewis Des Moines c. 1880

**Great Grandfather Charles HV Lewis Pharmacy in
Los Angeles c early 1900's**

**Great grandmother pharmacist Lydia Cram Lewis
Los Angeles c. 1900**

Grandfather Ray Lewis Sr. c 1920's enjoying the beach

Grandmother "Maymie" Vera-May Cooper
Venice c. 1910

Vera-May Cooper Venice c. 1915

Maymie c. 1916

Vera May center with chums c. 1916

Donna's mother, Dorothy Lewis (McIntyre). C. 1947. She painted this car by hand.

Donna's father Ray Lewis
4411 Ocean Front 1947

Ken and Donna engaged 1963

Foundation being poured at 4411 Ocean Front Walk c.1968

Ken was helping build front house of 4411, 1968

**Donna, expecting Julina, poses in front of 2909 Ocean Front Walk.
Spring 1968. Note no bike path**

Donna with Julie and Rick 1969 Venice

Donna with Rick and Julie visiting. Nov. 1969. With black lab Ginger and lab Taffy.

Donna and Ken Friess Family 2018

References

Primary Sources – Interviews

Breurer, Manya, interview. 1994. Camp Oswego. Videotaped. Accessed May 12, 2020.

Printed interview. Manya Breurer. *Interview with Safe Haven. Refugee. OH. 284. Penfield Library Special Collections. Suny. Oswego.* Accessed May 15, 2020.

Author Interviews

Christine Baumgartner, in person. April, 2020.

Charlie Clifton, in person. May 28, 2020

John Clifton, in person. May 28, 2020

Charlie Clifton, follow-up telephone. May 29 - June 10, 2020

John Clifton, follow-up telephone, May 29, 2020. Via text, June 2020.

Ken Friess, in person, multiple conversations. April – July, 2020.

Dee Dee Lewis Keel, multiple email and text conversations. April – July 2020.

Charles H. Lewis, Ed.D. multiple conversations. April – June, 2020.

Jacqueline Lewis, DDS. Telephone and email. April-July, 2020.

Dorothy Lewis McIntyre, April - June, 2020. Multiple conversations.

Renee and Marc Perlman, telephone. May 15, 2020. Follow-up via email. May 24, 2020.

Diana Lewis Starr, multiple communications. May-July, 2020.

Starr, Richard, email. June 10, 2020.

Sallie Jac Shafer, telephone July 1, 2020.

Primary Sources – Five Field Trips

Site visits: Marina del Rey, The boardwalk at Windward Avenue, Muscle Beach, Playa Vista, Ballona Creek Bridge, Playa del Rey, Ballona Creek Trail, Homes on Grand Canal, Marina Peninsula, Nick's Market, Multiple visits to Oakwood, the Binoculars Building, Gehry's home in Santa Monica, Santa Monica High School, Santa Monica College, Venice High School, Ocean Park condominiums, Ocean Park Beach, Venice Post Office, Venice Canals, Brooks Avenue, Westminster Park, Abbot Kinney Boulevard, The Kinney-Tabor Home, First Baptist Church, Recreation Center in Oakwood, Homeless encampments, Store front on W. Washington Boulevard, 4411 Ocean Front Walk, 2909 Ocean Front Walk, 52 Brooks Avenue, and the Venice – Santa Monica Boardwalk, Baldwin Hills Oil Fields, Historic

Canals District, Historic Helms District, Culver Center.

Secondary Sources – References

Abcarian, Robin, "California Journal: They discover, they gentrify, they ruin: How 'progress' is wrecking Los Angeles neighborhoods." *Los Angeles Times. July 19, 2017.*

Alexander, Carolyn Elayne, *Images of America:* Venice*, California.*1999. Venice Historical Society. Arcadia Publishers. USA.

Arnold, Richard J. *Images of San Gabriel.* 2013. Arcadia Press. California.

Baldwin Hills-Los Angeles. https://en.wikpedia.org/wiki/baldwin_Hills-Los Angeles. Accessed 6/2/2020

Ballona Wetlands. Website. Accessed April-May, 2020.

Bardolph, Paige. "Traditonal Boat Building Helps Native Community Hone Ecological Knowledge." KCET. Video. November 5, 2019. www. KCET.org. Accessed July 7, 2020.

Blankstein, Andrew, and Winston, Richard. "Nineteen Arrested in Venice Gang Sweep." *Los Angeles Times*, February 20,2008.

Buchanan, Larry, Bui Quoctrung, and Patel, Jugal. Black Lives Matter May be the Largest Movement in U.S. History.. *The New York Times.* July 3, 2020

Elkind, Sarah S, "Oil in the City; The Fall and Rises of Oil Drilling in Los Angeles.*" Journal of American History*, Volume 99, Issue, June 20, 2012, Pages- 82-90.

Ellingson, Annlee. "Snap Inc. pulling up Stakes in Venice and heading to Santa Monica." March 3, 2018. *LA Biz-The Business Journal.*

Engelhardt, Zephryrin. *San Fernando Rey: The Mission of the Valley.* 1922. Franciscan herald Press. Chicago Illinois.

Friedersdor, Conor. "How Venice Beach Became a Neighborhood for the Wealthy." *The Atlantic.* July 24, 2017.

Friess, Donna L. *Whispering Waters: Historic Weesha and the Settling of Southern California. 1998.* HIH Publishing: California.

Frist, Gary. *The Mirage Factory: Illusion, Imagination and the Invention of Los Angeles.* Crown Publisher: 2018. New York.

Garner, Scott, "Venice compound with historic past hits the market for $5.8 million." *Los Angeles Times,* August 16, 2016.

Garner, Scott. "Neighborhood Spotlight: Marina del Rey Sets a Course for Comeback." *Los Angeles Times,* August 25, 2016

Grace, Michael. "The Other S.S. Rex- a gambling ship off Santa Monica, California in the 1930's and early 1940's. Posted by Grace from *Time Magazine, August 19, 1946.*

Gruber, Ruth. True Drama film. *Haven.* 2001. Prime Time Emmy Award. *Prime TV.* Accessed April, 2020.

Hanney, Delores. *The Lure of the Sea: Venice Vignettes.* 2012. Createspace. North Charleston. S.C.

Heinman, Jim. *Los Angeles: Portrait of a City.* 2013. Taschen. Printed in Slovakia.

Kinney, Abbot, biography. www. Westland.net. Venice History/ articles/ Kinney. accessed 5/10/2020

Kudler, Adria Glick. "Super Producer Joe Silver Buying, Saving Venice Post Office." June 11, 2012. *LA Curbed. Com.* Accessed May 17, 2020.

History of Ballona Wetlands. https://www.ballonafriends.org/history-of-ballona-wetlands. 5/24/2020

Jackson, Helen Hunt. American Poet. *Wikipedia*. Accessed 5/14/2020.

Los Angeles. Careers. Accessed, June 13, 2020.

Marina del Rey Historical Society Website. May, 2020.

Masters, Nathan. "The Lost Canals of Venice of America. April 5, 2013. KCET. Lost LA Video Series.

Masters, Nathan. "Lost Wetlands of Los Angeles." February, 2012. KCET. Los LA Video Series.

Old Restaurants (in Los Angeles).com accessed June 30, 2020

Robinson, Alicia. "From drilling to swellings: Housing plans for Brea's last big oil field move forward." *Orange County Register*. December 28, 2019.

Shevitz, Amy Hill. Israel at the Shore of the Sea: Jewish Space and Place in Venice, California. *Southern California Quarterly, 2001.*

Smith, James. R. *The Gentrifying of Paradise: Resistance and Removal in 21st Century Venice California.*2019. Venice West Publishers, Venice, CA.

Spitzzeri, Paul. "No Place Like Home: The Abbot Kinney Residence at Kinneloa, CA 1883." 1/22/2018. The homestead museum. *Work press.com/2018*. Accessed 5/12/2020.

Staff writers. The Rise of Silicon Beach. www. *Discover Los Angeles*. March 14, 2019.

The Tongva. *Santa Monica Audubon Society*. Official website. Smbasblog.com. Pacific Palisades, Ca. Accessed 5/26/2020.

Venice Breakwater: *Tourist Attractions in Los Angeles*. Accessed 6/10/2020

The Venice Canals. History of the Venice, California Canals and the Creation of Venice of America. *Venice Walking Tour*. Accessed online. April, 2020. Californiathroughmylens.com

Venice Canals. Historic Landmark of Los Angeles. *Photo tour*. Accessed. April 2020.

Venice 13 Gang. https://en.m.wikipedia.org/wiki/Venice-13. 6/1/2020 www.EA.com.

Venice Timeline. 1970-199. https://www.wwestland.net/venicehistory/articles/1970. htm. accessed 5/30/2020.

Venice Historical Society Website. April, 2020.

www.cruiselinehistory.com. Accessed May 28, 2020.

Index

O

P

R

S

Made in the USA
Las Vegas, NV
12 January 2021